INSIDE NUREMBERG PRISON

INSIDE NUREMBERG PRISON

Hitler's Henchmen Behind Bars & the German Jew

HELEN FRY

THISTLE
PUBLISHING

This edition published in 2015 by:

Thistle Publishing
36 Great Smith Street
London
SW1P 3BU
www.thistlepublishing.co.uk

ISBN-13: 978-1-910670-33-0

Dedicated to the memory of
Lina and Berthold Triest
who perished in Auschwitz

"If you were to say of these men that they are not guilty,
it would be as true to say that there had been no war,
there were no slain, there has been no crime."
US Chief Justice Jackson, Nuremberg Trial, 1946

CONTENTS

AUTHOR'S NOTE

This is a book about life in Nuremberg Prison at the end of the Second World War and the drama that unfolded with the top Nazi leaders during their year behind bars during the trial itself. It is told primarily through the eyes Howard Triest, originally a German Jew who, in an unexpected twist of fate, fought on the frontline as an American soldier and became the only German-Jewish translator to the psychiatrists in prison. His true identity remained hidden from the defendants and led to an extraordinary turn of events.

During the course of my work, I have interviewed many veterans in Howard Triest's situation – refugees from Nazi Germany and Austria who fought for the Allies in the war. Most have coped with the trauma by building a wall of silence around the past and never speaking of it to their families. The silence protected them from having to confront intense trauma and deep emotional pain. It soon becomes apparent that Howard is one of those veterans who has always readily talked about the past. His openness makes the interviewing process easier.

He seems unoffended by the very direct personal questions and displays a relaxed approach to the whole experience, although offering a conscious and proud perspective of his unique role at Nuremberg. Today, there is a certain pride for him that he succeeded without breaking down in front of the defendants. In a cheerful manner, he explains that the Allies had just won the war and he was assigned to Nuremberg in the full knowledge that he was part of the victorious forces. He was entering the prison cells with his freedom, while the defendants sat behind bars. He knew, and so did they, that they would hang for their crimes. Howard had his life ahead of him; the defendants were effectively at the end of theirs.

I find myself compelled by Howard's story. Here is a man who got as close as one possibly could to the surviving leaders of the Nazi government on a daily basis and yet bore no bitterness or desire for revenge. I wanted to hear his anger, feel his hatred but it is surprisingly not there. There is no outpouring of trauma and hate. For him it is as simple now as it was then: justice would have to be done if Germany was to be rebuilt. I find it hard to believe it is this simple. How can he be so forgiving? I am driven to find answers to deep questions and to understand what makes him tick.

Much of Howard's life was narrated in a logical and detached way, and that comes across in the book. Stories were often shot through with frank humour. The emotion lay buried deep and never once surfaced in the interviews. One question remained unanswered for me: had Howard ever been able to grieve the loss of his parents? Or had he buried the emotion so deep to protect his sanity? His initial response is to say that it is a complicated one. Then after a pause, he replied: 'every time I step inside a shower... which is every day... I think of the showers in Auschwitz, the showers that killed my parents.'

Inside Nuremberg Prison provides a unique eye-witness account of those days out of the public eye whilst the world waited for justice to be played out in the courtroom.

PART 1

A MATTER OF JUSTICE

Preface

THE LETTER

August 1942, Vichy France

IN THE UNBEARABLY hot, cramped carriage of the freight train the attractive but now frail forty-three year old Lina Triest squeezed through the Jewish prisoners towards the window. Reaching into her pocket, she pulled out an envelope, stood on tiptoe and tossed it through the small opening at the top of a window. The summer breeze briefly caressed her fingertips. Her terrified, desolate eyes strained to see the envelope land at the side of the track. What hope had she of it reaching her 'go-between' in Switzerland? The round-up six months earlier of foreign Jews living in France seemed a distant memory.

Lina turned away from the window and made her way back to her husband. Berthold looked desperately ill. She clutched his hand, wondering if he would survive the journey. The train carrying its human cargo sped on through the French countryside, heading from Les Milles in the south towards Camp Drancy in the north on the outskirts of Paris. Nothing was going to protect Lina and Berthold from the fate that awaited Europe's Jews...

Nearly three years later, in April 1945, and a world away, the American 5th Corps was stationed in Germany having fought its way from the Normandy beaches through Belgium and Holland. Lina and Berthold's twenty-two year old son, Sergeant Howard Triest, had been with the Military Intelligence Interpretation team of 5th Corps for ten months. He was part of the mighty war machine that was on the verge of defeating the Third Reich. Howard was back on German soil for the first time in six years since forced to flee Munich on the very eve of the war. For him, it felt like pay-back time on a massive scale. The final defeat was just days away. Nazi forces were collapsing all over Germany and the Russians were heading for Berlin. The last time he stood on European soil was in 1940 as a seventeen year old emigrating to the safety of America. Howard was confident he would see his father, mother and sister, Margot, again in a matter of weeks.

Growing up in Munich, Howard had seen enough to know that they, like all Jews, were in danger but not enough to understand that Adolf Hitler would stop at nothing to expand the borders of the Third Reich. The anti-Jewish laws and persecutions of 1930s Germany, and 1938 Austria, set Germany on a path towards the Final Solution – the annihilation of six million Jews and five million others. But who could have known in 1940 as Howard left for America that within two years Hitler would give his orders for the total destruction of European

Jews? Churchill, Roosevelt and even Stalin hadn't thought it would come to that.

Now with the Third Reich on the verge of collapse, Howard received orders that he was being transferred to Nuremberg, a posting that would bring him into daily contact with Hitler's henchmen in their prison cells. How would this German Jew react to being so close to pure evil, including the men who sent his own parents to the gas chambers of Auschwitz? Was reconciliation with Germany possible in the light of such nationwide complicity?

Seventy years later, Howard is the only surviving witness to those prison interviews. The psychiatric team in the prison, Dr Kelley, Dr Gilbert and Dr Goldensohn, and the prison commandant Colonel Andrus have all since died. Now living in Florida and in his nineties, not a day goes by when he does not think about the past. But is not with melancholic sadness or acrimony. Over seven decades, he has reflected on his time at Nuremberg and his own personal loss. Having worked with the psychiatrists for so long, he became conscious then of his own need to deal with deep psychological scars. The result of this self-awareness is a man who lacks bitterness or resentment. His story is chilling, yet emotional, and one which reveals a man of great dignity.

CHAPTER ONE

NUREMBERG PRISON

"The only right way to punish these twenty-one defendants was to put them into the death camps and subject them to the same treatment they gave millions of others. But we couldn't do that as civilized people." Howard Triest.

AT THE END of the Second World War, twenty-two surviving members of Hitler's government were behind bars in Nuremberg Prison, awaiting trial for their part in the most heinous crimes in history. The accused were Hermann Goering, Rudolf Hess, Julius Streicher, Joachim von Ribbentrop, Robert Ley, Field Marshal Keitel, Ernst Kaltenbrunner, Alfred Rosenberg, Hans Frank, Admiral Raeder, Wilhelm Frick, Baldur von Schirach, Franz von Papen, Fritz Sauckel, Artur Seyss-Inquart, Baron von Neurath, Hans Fritzsche, Walther Funk, Hjalmar Schacht, Albert Speer, Admiral Doenitz and General Jodl. The latter three were arrested in the enclave of Flensburg, the final seat of Nazi government on the German-Danish border.

The trial was scheduled to open in the third week of November. Before it did, the prison would witness much drama and unpredictability from the defendants. While the prosecution team carefully assembled and prepared the evidence, there was little doubt in the minds of the staff at the prison that few, if any, of the accused would walk out of the jail as free men. Strict controls were in place for Allied personnel entering and leaving the premises.

The choice of the city of Nuremberg was deliberate and symbolic. Once the scene of mass rallies and displays of Nazi strength during the 1930s, this was the end game for a regime that Adolf Hitler believed would last for a thousand years. The trial was taking place a just a short distance from the vast stadium of their halcyon Nuremberg Rallies. This was also the city of the infamous Nuremberg Laws of 1935 that deprived Jews of their civil liberties. It now stood in the American sector of Allied-occupied Germany as a test to international justice. Nuremberg was about to deliver the final deathblow to the Nazi regime.

Beyond the walls of Nuremberg's Palace of Justice where the trial was about to convene, Allied occupying forces were getting on with the task of restoring democracy to a country that had lived for thirteen years under Nazi tyranny and brutality. While physical structures were being rebuilt, democracy reinstated to German media and all traces of Nazi ideology removed from every aspect of post-war institutions and civic life, the world was about to hold to account those responsible for crimes against humanity on a scale never witnessed before.

The indictment, the crimes for which the defendants were being tried, was read in German to each of the defendants in their cells. That task fell to British officer, Major Airey Neave of MI9, a branch of the British Secret Service. Neave had been the first escapee from the security prison Colditz, having been captured in action during the war.

Neave wrote in his memoirs that he felt intense anger when so physically close to these men of men and admits that he would not have been an ideal candidate as a translator to enter the cells every day with the psychiatrists.

After the indictment was read, Hermann Goering became particularly gloomy, though the charges were not totally unexpected for him. Rudolf Hess wanted to defend himself, but was advised against it. For someone so unbalanced and displaying odd behaviour in custody, Hess certainly appeared to understand the indictment.

THE OPENING OF THE TRIAL

On 20 November 1945, twenty-one defendants flanked by US guards were brought along the covered walkway from the prison cells, up the stairs, through a door behind the prisoners' box and into the courtroom. There was no escaping their fate. If any of them had tried to make it beyond the prison walls, the German people were in no mood to harbour these war criminals. The grotesqueness of their crimes was still unfolding to a horrified and scarred surviving people. Suicide was the only way to avoid justice and that seemed unlikely given the close twenty-four hour guard over each defendant. However, the tight security did not prevent defendant, Robert Ley from taking his own life before the trial even began.

British barrister and politician, Sir Hartley Shawcross, led the British prosecution team; Chief Justice Jackson the American team. The courtroom in the Palace of Justice had already been extended to accommodate the large dock, visitors' gallery and a separate area for the international press. Prisoners were led into the dock and seated in two rows. Hermann Goering, who had assumed leadership of the others, took the first seat at the end of the front row of prisoners; behind stood guards of the US forces. The accused shuffled in their seats, put on headphones to be able to hear the whole proceedings in translation as a hush descended on the packed courtroom. There was not a single empty seat in the visitors' gallery; and the specially constructed press box filled with journalists and reporters who would bring to the world the full extent of the evil for which the defendants were standing trial.

In the coming months, the world would hear and see for the first time graphic images of atrocities committed in the concentration camps flashed on screens in the courtroom. It would cause universal shock. In Howard's experience of living through the trial, he could see that nothing could prepare the world for the unrelenting genocide that was revealed by the prosecuting team. The little evidence that had been reported throughout the war seemed to have been largely dismissed as exaggerated Allied propaganda. Now the world would see the incontrovertible evidence.

The trial was a first and a test for international law and co-operation. Four charges never tried before in a court of law were being brought before the defendants:

- Count One – The Common Plan or Conspiracy: conspiracy to commit crimes alleged in other accounts.
- Count Two – Crimes against Peace: planning to wage war

- Count Three – War Crimes: ill-treatment and murder of civilians and prisoners of any country before or during the war.
- Count Four – Crimes against Humanity: murder, extermination, racial and political persecution or enslavement before or during the war.

Twenty-four defendants were indicted, only twenty-one made an appearance in court. Hitler's private secretary Martin Bormann was tried in absentia. Robert Ley had already committed suicide in his prison cell. Industrialist Gustav Krupp, who had built a large fuse factory at Auschwitz where Jews were worked to exhaustion and then sent to their deaths in the gas chambers, was declared physically unfit to stand trial. Hitler, Goebbels and Himmler were already dead, and Adolf Eichmann and Dr Josef Mengele had fled to places unknown, presumed to be somewhere in South America. The defendants all pleaded 'not guilty' to the charges laid before them. Goering was the first to do so. The others followed suit.

On 21 November 1945, the day after the trial opened, US prosecutor Chief Justice Jackson gave his four-hour defining opening address in which he said:

> 'The privilege of opening the first trial in history for crimes against the peace of the world imposes a grave responsibility. The crimes which we seek to condemn and punish have been so calculated, so malignant and so devastating that civilization cannot tolerate their being ignored because it

cannot survive their being repeated. The four great nations, flush with victory and stunned with injury stay the hand of vengeance and voluntarily submit their captive enemies to the judgment of the bar in one of the most significant tributes that power has ever paid to reason... We have no purpose here to incriminate the whole German people. Hitler did not achieve power by a majority vote but seized it by an evil alliance of revolutionaries, reactionaries and militarists. You will hear today and in the days ahead of the enormity and horror of their acts. The prosecution will give you undeniable proofs of these incredible events – and I count myself as one who received during the war most atrocity tales with suspicion or scepticism.'

The existence of this trial had by no means been certain during the war. Although the four Allied powers of Britain, the United States, France and the Soviet Union were united in agreeing that mistakes made at the end of the First World War should be avoided at all cost, they disagreed on how it should be achieved. They acknowledged that forcing Germany to pay huge reparations by the Treaty of Versailles in 1919 had led to a humiliated country on the brink of economic collapse. High inflation had paved the way for Adolf Hitler to come to power in 1933. However, the powers disagreed on the existence of an international trial for war criminals.

As early as October 1943, the Soviet Foreign Minister, Vyacheslav Molotov, had suggested that the Nazi leader should be subjected to war crimes trials. The Russians were disappointed that Britain, who had held Rudolf Hess from 1941, had been unwilling during the war itself to bring him immediately to trial but instead decided to focus all efforts on winning the war.

On 1 November 1943, the Allies agreed in principle in the Moscow Declaration that that major war criminals would face war crimes but no outline given on whether there would be a special trial or executions. At the Tehran Conference in late November, early December 1943, Stalin suggested to British Prime Minister Churchill and US President Roosevelt that around 50,000 of Germany's armed forces should be arrested and executed with the express aim of breaking the military might of the Third Reich. Churchill objected to the scale of the proposed mass executions. Later that evening, Stalin said he was only joking, but even so he had planted a seed that mass executions were an option.

During 1944, Churchill and Roosevelt were of the opinion that certain named Nazi war criminals should be executed without trial. Britain had argued that once caught, top Nazi war criminals should be executed immediately because their guilt was incontestable. Stalin appeared to agree until he rescinded and told them in October 1944 that there should be a trial, if for no other reason than to assure the world that the Allies as victors were not exacting revenge. Stalin's motives in suggesting this may have been twofold: to redeem the West's view of him since he had liquidated millions of his own people, and because he could use the trial as a propaganda tool. The Americans came to see that summary executions were not appropriate and a trial more advisable.

The situation took a turn with the death of President Roosevelt on 12 April 1945. Roosevelt was succeeded by Harry Truman who immediately endorsed the Soviet demands for a full trial. For the trial to succeed, the four powers had to come to agreement on its form, the charges to be brought, which war criminals would be tried and the location. Each country had a different judiciary system but eventually the British and Americans worked out a compromise on the proceedings. Certain civic rights in the US judiciary system would be denied the accused i.e. calling on the Fifth Amendment (the right to remain silent and not answer a question). The defendants would have to answer questions posed to them by the legal teams during the trial.

With the agreements made, by the time the trial opened there was no doubt in the minds of the four occupying powers of the purpose of the court. The legal teams were there to ensure that Nazism would never rise again and justice would be executed. In the words of British Prosecutor Sir Hartley Shawcross, it was: 'first, retribution for those who committed the crimes; second, that right will prevail and thirdly, the individual shall transcend the state.' He went on to famously say: 'There comes a point when a man must refuse to answer to his leader if he is also to answer to his own conscience.'

Shawcross was concerned that the trial should not be seen by the outside world as reprisal by the victors. Instead he emphasized the rule of law so the trial would keep its integrity. Much of the trial of course was taken up with endless complex legal statements and arguments which were largely meaningless and mundane for all those present except the legal teams. The defendants looked to Hermann Goering for advice at key moments during the trial. Goering resented anything which meant he was not the centre of attention and that applied to the courtroom. In his eyes, he had to have the best seat in the court. He disapproved of the other defendants taking a lead role or stealing the limelight from him.

The daily running of the trial relied on fluent German speakers. These were drawn largely from those German-refugees who had once fled the regime and were now serving in the British and American forces. They were posted to Nuremberg as translators and interpreters to help the justice system in the months preceding the trial and during it. One of those émigrés was Howard Triest whose unique story follows. His life up until 1945 essentially parallels the birth and death of Nazism. It is a tale of two cities: Munich and Nuremberg, cities that symbolised the birth and death of the Third Reich. Munich – the birthplace and cradle of Nazism. Nuremberg – the death place of Nazism.

Munich had nursed the nascent political aspirations of Adolf Hitler and his henchmen. In November 1923, nine months after Howard Triest was born in the city, it witnessed Hitler's failed Putsch when he and his closest circle attempted to overthrow the Bavarian government. Amongst the circle were Rudolf Hess and Hermann Goering who would later stand trial in Nuremberg. Munich was also once home to Heinrich Himmler, Hitler's right-hand man who masterminded the liquidation program of the Jews. After the failed Putsch, Hitler was arrested and spent a year in prison where, with the aid of Rudolf Hess, he wrote his infamous book *Mein Kampf*. Nuremberg, once the symbol of Nazi might in the 1930s, became the city where justice was ultimately executed and where Howard witnessed first-hand the final downfall of the regime.

What follows is first a detailed look at Howard's early life and how the Nazi regime impacted upon it to understand what he lived through and the poignancy of the events which eventually led to his posting to Nuremberg. It is also in stark ironic contrast to the situation he was to find himself during his time at Nuremberg Prison. Howard's position at Nuremberg gave him an unprecedented insight into life behind bars for the former leaders of the Nazi government. What unfolded in those cells would have seemed implausible if written as fiction. This is a true story and one which sheds light on a little known aspect of the Nazi leaders during the final year of their lives.

PART 2

HOWARD'S STORY

CHAPTER TWO

MUNICH AND THE HITLER YEARS

H OWARD TRIEST'S STORY began in Munich as Hans Heinz Triest on 29 March 1923 in a former painter's apartment at 2-4 Manhardt Strasse. His mother, Lina, and father, Berthold, had married the previous year on 23 April. Berthold was a proud veteran of the First World War, having fought in the German forces for four years in the rank of Feldlazarett Inspektor, for which he was awarded the Iron Cross. The experience of war left its scars and he rarely spoke about his experiences. After the war, Berthold set up a business *Neumeyer & Triest* in Munich with Mr Neumeyer. They purchased a factory at 2-4 Mueller Strasse and manufactured gentlemen's clothing, dressing gowns, pyjamas and shirts. The factory employed around 150 people.

When Howard was 18 months old, his parents moved from Manhardt Strasse to 53 Reitmorstrasse in the suburbs of Munich. His sister Margot was born there on 19 April 1929. Howard and Margot grew up in an upper-middle class environment in which their parents employed a cook and lived in a smart apartment. They were raised as

Reform Jews and only attended services for the High Holy Days. Their parents saw themselves as patriotic Germans. As a largely assimilated German Jewish family, Berthold and Lina taught their children to respect their German culture and roots. He recalled:

'German Jews were always German first, Jews second. Our family was no exception. My father loved Germany and was deeply loyal to his country. It was his homeland until the Nazis forced us out. He and my mother share the same birthday, although they were born in different years. My mother was born Lina Westheimer on 8 January 1899 in Karlsruhe; my father in Bamberg on 8 January 1886. We never discussed the religious upbringing of my parents or grandparents. My maternal grandmother ate kosher meat but had other meat in the house for her son Kurt, my uncle, who ate anything.'

Berthold was a reserved man by nature. Lina was a beautiful, outgoing and vivacious woman who enjoyed entertaining.

Howard's earliest childhood memory was of starting school. The first four years were spent at the Gebele School, a German state school. It was a twenty-five minute walk across a large bridge over the picturesque river Isar. Sometimes, his father's chauffeur Jungmeyer took the young Howard to school if his father did not need the car for work. Jews were a minority in Howard's school. On occasion, the 1-hour religious studies lesson was provided by a local rabbi. From the Gebele School, Howard attended the Wilhelms Gymnasium where he learnt Latin and Greek. After a year, he transferred to a Real Gymnasium for modern languages where he added English and French to his repertoire. Then he attended the Hoehere Handelsschule where he added subjects such as typing and shorthand to his knowledge of modern languages.

It was a life sheltered, free from the worries and political instability within Germany in the 1920s. At that time, nothing shattered the idyll that characterised Howard's childhood or that of other Jews living in Germany. No one foresaw in those early years that within a decade the world would be turned upside and Germany's Jews hunted down and persecuted.

In the 1920s, Germany was still reeling from the effects of the 1914-18 war and the subsequent Treaty of Versailles (1919) in which Allies America, France, Britain and Russia forced Germany to pay huge reparations and imposed restrictions on future military rearmament. Germany and much of Europe was suffering the effects of hyper-inflation. 'Milk sold for a million marks,' comments Howard. Germany not only had to cope with hyper-inflation but the financial repercussions of Allied war reparations. The subsequent humiliation led to a nation with a severe loss of pride. The German people yearned for change. The Treaty of Versailles held within it the seeds for Adolf Hitler's rise to power in the 1930s and another world war. He promised to restore Germany's pride, build a great nation again and a world without inflation and poverty. All this was soon to impact on Howard's childhood.

LIFE UNDER NAZISM

At the age of ten, Howard experienced the full brunt of the Nazi regime. On 30 January 1933, Adolf Hitler came to power in Germany. The majority of ordinary Germans embraced his leadership because of his persuasive promises of jobs at a time of mass unemployment and high inflation. The new leader raised Germany's hopes by injecting a much yearned-for pride back into the nation. Howard's parents and wider family (his aunts and uncles), like many Jews at that time, could not believe it had happened. Howard knew from the adults around him that Hitler's new power was bad news, but had no real comprehension of why. Although his parents knew the situation was grave, they held to the not uncommon view amongst Germany's Jews that it would all blow over. They believed that Hitler would not last.

Like much of Europe, Germany was in a state of political upheaval but it was seen as a temporary state of affairs. Governments in Europe generally were not very secure at that time so, in those early days, the Triests felt they had nothing to fear in the long-term from the Nazi regime. Perhaps Lina, more than any other family member, realized the gravity of the situation because she hired an English expatriate to tutor Howard and Margot in the English language. When later in 1940 Howard found himself living in America, he was able to be understood because of his basic knowledge of English from the tutor.

On 23 March 1933, Hitler's power was extended further when the German parliament passed a Bill enabling him to rule by decree. With rapid effect, Hitler turned Germany into a one-party Nazi state. This almost absolute control was to have devastating consequences for the Jews of Europe over the next thirteen years. As Jews, Howard's family would find themselves irrevocably caught up in these events. For the young Howard the political situation largely passed over his head in those early days because he did not see how it would affect him personally. However one event during 1933 was particularly memorable. He recalls:

'My mother, father, sister and I were having a day out beside a lake with extended family. Some of the adults began to remark that Hitler had just become Chancellor and had gained complete power. I remember this discussion because of their reaction to the news – they were all terribly upset. I didn't think much about it. I was more concerned about my toys, school and running around having a good time.'

The visible effects of the Nazi regime were now everywhere. Streets and squares in Munich were re-named. Nazi flags hung from buildings in the main streets, and Stormtroopers (SS) and *Sturm Abteilung* (SA) men carried out regular patrols. On 1 April 1933, the Nazis ordered a boycott of Jewish shops and businesses in Germany. Signs appeared saying 'this is a Jewish shop. You are not allowed to shop here'. On non-Jewish shops, signs read '*Juden sind unerwünscht*' (Jews not allowed here). The same signs eventually appeared on notices at public places like swimming pools, dental and medical practices and cinemas. Fortunately Berthold Triest's factory at 2-4 Mueller Strasse remained untouched at this time by the boycott of Jewish businesses.

Just seven days later, on 7 April 1933, a law was passed prohibiting Jews from practicing in the legal profession. This sparked the first wave of emigration of professional intellectual Jews from Germany to countries like Britain and America. Jewish intellectuals were targeted again when Minister of Propaganda Joseph Goebbels ordered the burning of so-called "undesirable" books on 10 May 1933. These included the works by leading figures like Karl Marx, Heinrich Heine and Sigmund Freud. In Berlin's university square, academics and students gathered to begin an action that would see the burning of at least 20,000 books. Such was the brainwashing of the German nation that most of the younger generation had no knowledge of what they were burning, having never read the books being cast ceremoniously into the flames.

Reality came closer to home for Howard when, two months later on 15 July 1933, his uncle Kurt Westheimer (his mother's brother) was arrested by the Gestapo at his place of work in Munich. Uncle Kurt worked for *Klaubers*, a Munich-based firm which manufactured ladies fine slips and gowns. A group of Gestapo officers arrived on site and demanded to speak to some of the employees. Kurt replied: "Not now. They're working. You can speak to them on their day off."

His reply was deemed anti-Nazi obstruction. He was immediately arrested and taken off to Dachau concentration camp, 7km north-west of Munich. The camp at Dachau, which had opened four months earlier in March 1933, was the first of Hitler's concentration camps. In the early days, it was used to intern political dissidents of the State and was intended as a deterrent to scare the German people into submission to the Nazi ideal. Over a number of years, the Commandant Theodor Eicke ran a brutal regime under squads of SS "Death head" units.

During its operational years until liberation by American forces on 29 April 1945, over 200,000 prisoners were incarcerated in the camp. At least 30,000 officially died there, although the figures are probably higher since many deaths went unrecorded. Conditions were deliberately harsh and brutal. Kurt's arrival is recorded in the *Zugangsbuch* (entry ledger). The records show that he was deployed to a prisoner roadworks unit in August and September 1933.

Kurt was one of the lucky ones who survived Dachau. He was finally released after approximately a year, although the archives at Dachau do not record the exact date of release. A year in the camp meant that even in freedom and only in his thirties, Kurt was unfit for proper work. Even if he could have worked, as a Jew he could no longer get a work permit. After his release Kurt did not speak about his time in the camp because if he had, he would have been re-arrested and sent back there. In 1935, he and his wife emigrated to America and settled in Detroit. He changed his name to Kurt West. 'It was lucky that he got out,' comments Howard, 'because if he had stayed, he would certainly not have survived the Holocaust.'

A MATTER OF SURVIVAL

Events for Germany's Jews deteriorated yet further in 1934 when German President Hindenburg died at the age of 86, thus paving the way for Adolf Hitler to grasp a tighter hold on power. Hitler was proclaimed 'Führer and Reichskanzler' [Chancellor]. With the death of Hindenburg, Hitler's power base was absolute. Nothing stood in his way. He embarked on a program of re-armament in direct contravention of the Treaty of Versailles.

By the following year, he had formed the Luftwaffe (the German air force) and introduced conscription for men between the ages of 18 and 45. There was worse news for German Jews when, in the summer of 1935, the Nuremberg Laws were passed. These racial laws forbade fraternization between Aryans and Jews, and Jews were no longer allowed to marry non-Jews or be seen together. Howard does not remember feeling frightened during this period, except on the odd occasion when there were raids in the neighbourhood: 'When there were searches by the SA and Gestapo, I would go to my bedroom and pull the covers over my head. I thought that if they came to us no one would see me under the bed sheet!'

However, as Howard soon discovered, he personally had an easier time under the Nazis. With his blond hair and blue eyes, he looked the perfect Aryan. Neither did he have an obviously Jewish surname. In his lederhosen he passed off as a nice German boy. The newspaper *Der Stürmer* was distributed everywhere depicting [supposedly] what a Jew looked like. Howard wandered around Munich freely and was never stopped by Gestapo, SS or Brownshirts. It highlighted the failure of the Nazi myth about being able to define who was a Jew. Ironically the same scenario would be played out during Howard's experience in the Nuremberg Prison eleven years later.

The only time Howard ever had issue with his Jewishness was at school but there again he was originally mistaken for an Aryan. On the first day at High School the children chose their seats in the classroom. Howard sat next to his Jewish friend:

'A couple of boys came over to me and said: "you don't want to sit next to that Jew." They didn't realize I was Jewish. I replied: "I am Jewish."

"Oh" they said and walked away. German schoolchildren were educated to be attuned to who was a Jew and what a Jew was supposed to look like.'

Even now Berthold Triest still believed that Hitler would not last, until one day an incident occurred which caused him to take his family immediately to Luxembourg. The family was returning from an afternoon outing in one of the parks outside Munich.

Howard overheard his parents speaking to his aunt and uncle. They seemed very excited and told Howard and his sister Margot that they would be leaving that night to stay with relatives in Luxembourg. No explanation was given. The family packed that night and left Germany. It was still possible then for Jews to travel and hold a passport then. It was only sometime later that Howard found out the reason for their hurried departure. His uncle Max's brother, Justin Brandeis (a bachelor), had had an affair with a non-Jewish woman, now forbidden under Nazi law. As a consequence, Brandeis was in hiding from the Gestapo and faced being thrown into prison or killed when caught. Berthold thought this could lead to repercussions for the rest of the family, hence his decision to leave his home and business and take his family to Luxembourg.

As a precaution, Max Brandeis and his wife Heddy also left with their two children (Walter and Ruth) for Belgium and never returned to Germany. Eventually, they were able to emigrate to Palestine with the help of friends who paid £5,000 (over a year's salary for some professions) to secure their emigration. Berthold kept the family in Luxembourg for a few days and then decided perhaps they ought to return to Munich because of his business. He still believed that one day things would get better for the Jews.

Howard recalls: 'No Gestapo officers were after us, so we returned to Munich. That was one of the mistakes he made. If we had stayed in Luxembourg my father would have lost his factory but kept his life.'

EXPANSION OF THE NAZI REGIME

The following summer of July 1936, there was a further erosion of the terms of the Treaty of Versailles when German troops were ordered to occupy the Rhineland. The area had been declared a de-militarized zone under the Treaty. While the political face of Germany was changing, Howard has happy memories of his early childhood and life under the Nazi regime, but that would soon change. Up until 1937, the family still enjoyed holidays in Italy and Karlsbad, a mineral spa in Czechoslovakia. The effects of the Nazi regime became much more noticeable to Berthold who began to see 'the writing on the wall', but it was becoming ever more difficult to get out. It was not a matter of just leaving everything behind and getting a ticket out.

Maybe deep down, Berthold still harboured an unrealistic hope that it would all change. Through all this, the young Howard and Margot still managed to live a relatively sheltered life from the effects of the Nazis until 1938. That was the year that everything changed and emigration was the only way out.

Fifteen years after Hitler wrote his vision for Germany in his book *Mein Kampf,* he fulfilled the next stage of his expansionist dream. On the night of 12 March 1938, he ordered a massive military force to cross the border into Austria and annex the country in what became known as the *Anschluss.* Two days later, he entered the capital Vienna in an impressive procession to messianic acclaim by the population. The anti-Jewish laws which had come to pass gradually in Germany over a number of years, and which the young Howard witnessed, came into immediate force for the Jews of Austria. He comments: 'The invasion of Austria was expected, a test of how England and France would react. They did not react and so Czechoslovakia would be next. I lived in Nazi Germany, a country where anything could happen at anytime. Hitler was an Austrian; it was a time of persecution and surprises. Nothing surprised us except the inaction of the West and Russia.'

Berthold's business began to decline rapidly that summer of 1938. Germans refused to trade with him because he was a Jew. Berthold tried to continue with the factory under increasingly difficult circumstances but it became quite hopeless. A once-thriving business began to rapidly decline under the boycott of his goods. Berthold's business partner, also a Jew, had died young and left his share of the business to Berthold. Now as sole owner of the business, Berthold had little choice but to sell. Howard is philosophical about his father's decision and says: 'Selling the business may have been a stroke of luck because if father had kept it, the Nazis would have destroyed it on *Kristallnacht* when they burned down Jewish businesses. At least he sold the factory and got some money for it.'

Berthold sold out to a man called Paul Povel whose family owned large weaveries in Nordhorn near the German/Dutch border. It was a distressing time to let go of the business which he and his partner had so successfully built up: 'The loss of the factory hit hard because my father became dismayed that it should have come to that. Again, he felt that as a patriotic German who had fought for Germany in the First World War surely this could not be happening to him. For the first time since Hitler came to power five years earlier, the Nazi regime was affecting our daily lives. Now it became a matter of survival.'

Having sold the business, there was no way Berthold could get other employment. He was 52 years old and Jewish. Time was spent feverishly contacting relatives and friends in the United States and other countries to try to get a visa for him and the family to get out of Germany. He realized now that they had to get out, but had probably left it too late:

> 'For so long my father thought someone would conquer Germany and make it all good again, but as time went by his hopes were shattered. If he had realized this earlier, maybe he would have got us out in 1934 or 1935 and not left it to the very last days. Then he and my mother would have survived the Holocaust.'

MUNICH AND 'PEACE IN OUR TIME'

In the autumn of 1938, all eyes again focused on Munich. From 22-24 September, British Prime Minister Neville Chamberlain flew to the city for face-to-face talks with Hitler in an attempt to avert war. The crisis concerned Hitler's expansionist eye on the Sudetenland, the areas along the Czech border which were mainly inhabited by ethnic Germans but belonged to Czechoslovakia. The emergency situation threatened to slide Europe into war.

The Munich talks were portrayed publicly as a last attempt to avert another war. All seemed hopeful when Chamberlain stayed at the Petersberg Hotel on the banks of the Rhine, not far from the city of Bonn. The German dictator stayed at his favourite hotel nearby, the Hotel Dreesen. The two leaders met at the Petersberg Hotel to discuss the deepening crisis over the Sudetenland. On the agenda was Hitler's threat to annex both the Sudetenland and Czechoslovakia. At the end of the month, on 30 September, after intense discussions, the Munich Agreement was signed by Germany, Britain, France and Italy which allowed for the German annexation of the Sudetenland. Czechoslovakia, which had not been part of the negotiations, viewed it as the ultimate betrayal.

Chamberlain returned to Britain and confidently declared: 'we have saved Czechoslovakia from destruction and Europe from Armageddon.' He promised the British people 'Peace in our Time.' Britain was not ready for another war, the memories of the horrors of the First World War and the loss of millions of lives still deeply affected the nation. However, one British politician and future Prime Minister was under no illusions about the implications of appeasement. Winston Churchill denounced the Agreement in the House of Commons, saying:

'We have suffered a total and unmitigated defeat … you will find that in a period of time which may be measured by years, but may be measured by months, Czechoslovakia will be engulfed in the Nazi regime. We are in the presence of a disaster of the first magnitude.'

In the end, Churchill was proved right. The Munich Agreement was a temporary appeasement and nothing but Hitler's relinquishing of his expansionist ideas could prevent Europe's descent into another world war.

Chapter Three

KRISTALLNACHT

WHILE BRITAIN SAVOURED the renewed optimism after the Munich Agreement, it was just a matter of weeks before the situation for Europe's Jews dramatically deteriorated. It was to affect the Triest family. At the end of October 1938, Hitler ordered the deportation of all Polish Jews from Germany to Zbuczyn, a border town in no-man's-land between Germany and Poland. The ramifications of this policy were soon to have devastating consequences when the actions of one man in Paris in early November gave Adolf Hitler the excuse he was looking for to unleash unrestrained violence and destruction against the Jews across the Third Reich.

On 7th November 1938, German diplomat Ernst vom Rath was shot in Paris by a Polish Jew Herschel Grynszpan in retaliation for the deportation of his family to Zbuczyn the previous month. Rath remained in a critical condition in a French hospital. Retribution came two days later and was exacted without mercy across the German Jewish community. On 9th November, vom Rath died from his wounds. That same day happened to be the fifteenth anniversary since Hitler's failed Putsch in Munich in 1923. Hitler used the death of vom Rath to carry out a tirade of violence against the Jews. His propaganda Minister Joseph Goebbels ordered a violent pogrom against the Jews of both Germany and Austria but claimed that these attacks were never orchestrated by the State.

During the day of 9th November and the night of 10th November, the Nazis unleashed Kristallnacht - the Night of Broken Glass. In towns, villages and cities across Germany and Austria, Stormtroopers and Brownshirts smashed the windows of Jewish businesses, looted Jewish shops and torched their buildings. Synagogues were set on fire and with it, the scrolls of the Torah (the first five books of Moses)

Over a thousand synagogues were destroyed that night, many becoming burnt-out shells of their former glory. The main synagogue in Munich's Herzog-Max-Strasse where Howard had celebrated his *bar mitzvah* at the age of 13 had already been razed to the ground by the Nazis in June that year to provide a car park. On Kristallnacht, other Munich synagogues were destroyed, including the orthodox synagogue Ohel Jacob on Herzog-Rudolf-Strasse. The synagogue near Berthold's factory remained untouched and still operates today. For those Jewish inhabitants who lived close or within the districts where the violence was carried out, it was a night of terror. The end result could not be determined except that it intensified panic for Jews trying to leave the country.

That night, many remained behind closed doors for fear of their lives, terrified that the Gestapo would come for the males in their household. Thousands of Jewish males were rounded up and sent to concentration camps. In total, nearly a hundred Jews were killed, with 25,000 arrested and sent to concentration camps. That night was an ominous sign of worse to come for Europe's Jews. If ever they were in doubt about Hitler's power to last as Chancellor of Germany-Austria, the actions that night proved them wrong. Adolf Hitler had unprecedented hold on power and had singled them out, although the full policy of the Final Solution was not formalized until 1942.

THE RIVER ISAR

Then aged fifteen and still living in Munich, Howard knew nothing of the events of Kristallnacht until the following morning. The Triests lived in a suburb away from the area where the violence occurred and were completely oblivious to the horror being perpetrated in the centre of Munich. They walked the short distance to a tree-lined path along the river Isar which Berthold knew would be deserted. They walked around the park for some time. Then Berthold came across a business acquaintance and chatted by the river for a while about the events of the previous night. It was then that Berthold learned more about the destruction of the synagogues and Jewish businesses and that his old factory escaped damage because it was no longer owned by a Jew.

Howard took it all in and listened silently. Finally, the men parted. Howard glanced back and saw two Gestapo approaching the acquaintance and arresting him. That day is a vivid today for Howard as it was in 1938:

'We continued walking and were passed by SS officers. My father and I were not arrested because we did not look Jewish. Also, my father was wearing a miniature emblem Iron Cross from the First World War that was issued to German veterans. It was a replica of the real one he had been given. He wore it that day to signify he was a German war veteran and that he had fought for Germany. He felt that if he had fought in the war, how could anyone say he wasn't a German? I still believe it was my father's Iron Cross that saved us that day.'

Howard and his father spent the rest of the day between different addresses so the Gestapo or SS could not catch up with them after failing to pick them up at their own apartment. They walked to his father's sister who was a widow with no males in the house except Howard's old grandfather who was in his 80s. They knew they would be safe there. After a while Berthold telephoned Lina and told her to meet them at another address which belonged to the aunt's sister. Howard recalls:

'We figured the police wouldn't call if there were no males registered at a particular address. We managed to get through the day without being arrested like other Jewish males. We finally returned home that evening and learned from our maid that no one had called to arrest us. Our family doctor who was also Jewish came over to our apartment to see how we were.'

The day after Kristallnacht, Berthold asked one of Howard's aunts to call at the apartment because he had an urgent task. He did not want anything in the place that resembled a weapon if it was raided by the Gestapo. From a cupboard, he took out a dagger and helmet from his days in the army in the First World War and gave them to her. She hid them under her coat, walked down to the River Isar and threw them in.

A few nights later, the Triest family received a knock at the door. SA troops stood on the doorstep ready to search the apartment. Howard's mother told them that her husband was extremely sick in bed. They pushed their way in, searched the apartment but mercifully left Berthold alone. Books which they deemed anti-Nazi were confiscated, including one called *The Whole Complete Marriage*. In their view, there was no such thing as a complete marriage.

During the search, Howard recognized one of the SA men as living only a block away from them. He recalled: 'From our balcony we could see his balcony. I never did find him after the war or what happened to him. It is possible that he died fighting for the Nazis.'

A MATTER OF TIME

In the immediate aftermath of Kristallnacht, it was dangerous for Jews to go out for fear of attack or arrest. Howard somehow felt that he would be fine because he did not look Jewish. A couple of days after Kristallnacht, he ventured out dressed in his lederhosen. He was desperate to buy a new autograph book and believed, as before, that he would be safe because of his Aryan looks. Maybe it was a little foolhardy because Jews were forbidden to use public transport, go to the movies or into certain stores. If he had been caught, the consequences would not bear thinking about. There was one particular shop where he could buy the book he wanted. With confidence he walked into town and succeeded. He returned home safely, but around him he did witness Jews being arrested.

After Kristallnacht, Jews were complete outcasts in the eyes of the regime and had no rights in Germany. They were no German citizens. Jewish passports were withdrawn to be stamped with a red J for *Juden*. Jewish males had 'Israel' added in front of their name and women the name 'Sarah'. With a J in their passports it would not be possible for the Triests to go on holiday abroad anymore even if they had wanted to. Kristallnacht was *the* turning point when the fifteen-year old Howard fully realized the implications of the Nazi regime and that things could only get worse for the Jewish community. Although he still did not feel that anything terrible would ever happen to him personally, the events of that night left a lifelong indelible mark of insecurity: 'Although I personally never suffered any attacks by the Nazis, since that terrible night I have been left with the feeling of immediacy and urgency – let's do such and such today because tomorrow may never come. It may be too late.'

In November 1938, the same thought was now on the mind of Howard's father as on that of every other Jew – how to get out of Germany. Every attention was given to trying to secure visas to leave the country urgently. any of Howard's school friends had already gone; others were arrested on Kristallnacht and released after a week or two in a concentration camp. They returned home with their heads shaven. Others never came back. Howard kept company with whatever Jewish teenagers were still left in Munich, most of them older than him.

Leaving Germany was still possible. The Triests could leave at any point as long as they had a visa, but it was getting a visa that was becoming increasingly difficult. The problem was being accepted by another country for emigration. Options were limited. Britain and Palestine had fixed quotas and America had a long waiting list. Berthold intensified efforts to get his family out. He looked to America for emigration. For that the family needed an Affidavit from relatives in the United States. Fortunately help came from a cousin in New York whom the family had not seen or spoken to for years. Contacting him became a necessity for survival.

By early 1939, Howard's family was on the waiting list for emigration to the United States; a list containing tens of thousands of names. Berthold knew it could take years for their number to come up and hopes soon faded of gaining a quick entry there. The Triests' number on the waiting list never actually came up while they were living in Germany.

In the spring of 1939, Hitler expanded the German borders by annexing the Sudetenland as agreed in the Munich Agreement. In March 1939, he occupied Czechoslovakia and it became ever clear that he did not want peace at any price. Later that summer, on 22 August 1939, Hitler told his Generals: 'the enemy did not expect my great determination. Our enemies are little worms. I saw them at Munich [reference to the Agreement]. Now Poland is in the position I wanted … I am only afraid some bastard will present me with a mediation plan at the last moment.'

There was no mediation plan but an ultimatum issued by British Prime Minister Chamberlain that if Hitler invaded Poland, then Britain would declare war on Germany.

As Europe slid ever closer to war, a wealthy and influential cousin in Luxembourg threw the Triest family a lifeline. The cousin succeeded in securing them a temporary visa to stay in Luxembourg until their America visas came through. The future was uncertain but at least there was hope.

CHAPTER FOUR

FREEDOM AND AMERICA

O N THE LAST day of August 1939, sixteen year old
Howard Triest left Nazi Germany ahead of his parents and sister Margot for Luxembourg. Their exit
permits were due any day. Howard was anxious about getting out of Germany safely, knowing that he risked being
arrested at any station where groups of SS officers ran-
domly searched trains. War was in the air as Howard travelled by train via Trier to the border with Luxembourg.
The train was packed with vacationers returning home
because of the threat of war. That evening Howard arrived
at Wasserbillig, a German border town with Luxembourg.
The next train into Luxembourg was not scheduled until
the following morning. That night he had no option but to
sleep on a bench on the station platform.

Dawn broke the next day to a very different world.
Overnight, Germany had invaded Poland. While Howard
had slept on a bench 'under the stars', the war had started
on the Polish border. Adolf Hitler had defied any warn-
ings from Britain and ordered his troops into Poland.

That morning of 1st September 1939, Howard passed
through German customs not yet aware of what had happened. Only when he crossed into Luxembourg did he

hear the announcement about Poland. He checked into a small hotel in Diekirch.

Two days later, on 3 September 1939, Britain declared war on Germany for its act of aggression against Poland. It was an uncertain and worrying time. Twenty-one years after the Great War, Europe was plunged once again into a bloody battle. This time it was a moral war: the apocalyptic fight between good and evil. In that fight, Britain initially stood alone against the might of Nazi Germany until America entered the war at the end of 1941 after the bombing of Pearl Harbour.

Howard's parents and sister were now trapped in Munich. Alone in Luxembourg, Howard telephoned home several times but had to be vigilant about what he said during the conversation. He was free, but his family was not. If he said something which his mother thought might compromise them, she hung up.

Then, at last, came the news that Howard had anxiously waited for. His parents and Margot were able to leave Germany on a temporary visa and join him in Luxembourg. Since it was forbidden for Jews to take currency out of Germany, Berthold and Lina carefully hid money in the backs of hair brushes. Ever resourceful and quick-thinking, Lina crammed toilet rolls into their suitcases. If they were searched at the border by SS officers, the toilet rolls would roll out as a distraction.

THE FAMILY REUNITES

Twelve days later, on a bright day in mid-September 1939, Berthold, Lina and Margot alighted at Diekirch station.

Howard was waiting on the platform. It was an emotional moment. Reunited, the family lodged together in a nearby guest house. Life in exile carried on for them in the relaxed knowledge that they would not be separated again. They had no immediate fears for the future. The days were spent on walks together and frequenting a tiny café. They enjoyed coffee and cakes and occasionally mixed with other refugee Jewish families.

Regular monthly payments in dollars were received by the Triests from a family member living in America. Dollars had a high value currency and enabled them to stay in Luxembourg and lead a pleasant life, largely sheltered from the daily reality of war. That continued until events took a dramatic turn eight months later.

As a new year dawned, 1940 witnessed Hitler's tightening stranglehold on Europe. At the beginning of April 1940, Berthold and Lina received a letter that their visas for emigration to the United States had finally come through and were ready for collection from an American Consulate. The nearest was Antwerp in Belgium. The family left Luxembourg and travelled together to Antwerp. With their visas safely secured, passage to America was within their grasp.

Back in Luxembourg, Berthold tried to arrange tickets on a ship for the United States but discovered that they only had sufficient money to purchase two tickets. It was a difficult dilemma. No one wanted to leave without the others. Berthold and Lina were particularly concerned that Howard should go on ahead because he was most at risk from being deported to a concentration camp if things went wrong. Margot was only eleven years old, so it was thought best that she stay with her parents until enough money had been saved for three tickets to America.

Howard bade farewell to his parents and Margot on the station platform at Diekirch in the knowledge that he would see them again very soon, even within a matter of a couple weeks. There were no tears or emotional farewells as he leant out of the train window. His mother leant in to kiss him. The only person Howard ever saw again was his sister, Margot.

JOURNEY TO FREEDOM

It was a rainy late afternoon on 26th April 1940 that Howard (then still as Hans Heinz Triest) boarded the ship *SS Pennland* at the port of Antwerp, bound for New York via Southampton. The ship was very crowded, mainly packed with people escaping Nazi Europe and the war. Howard was allocated a tiny cabin for two people but because of the overcrowding had to share it with four other passengers.

Once on board, Howard received a telegram informing him that his parents had finally received enough funds for their tickets to emigrate. They had successfully booked passage on SS Rotterdam, also a ship of the Holland-America line. They were due to sail from the port of Rotterdam on 10 May. The start of Howard's own journey on *SS Pennland* was interesting, as he comments:

'Just before we left Antwerp an interesting Russian character called Boris in his late 20s or early 30s boarded the ship. He was a friend of the Captain and had all kinds of connections. He became my table companion for the journey but he slept most of the day and got up very late. He smoked a lot and got me tasting my first cigarette. He was an interesting person, supposedly a relative of the Czar of Russia and had fought in the Spanish War. We became friends and I learnt to play shuffle board. For me it was a good crossing; although I was seasick a few times.'

The ship was scheduled to make one stop en route to New York and that was the port of Southampton on the south coast of England. Because the English Channel was mined it took ten days to reach Southampton from Antwerp. The *SS Pennland* stopped and anchored off the French coast at Dunkirk for several days before continuing to Southampton. It finally docked at Southampton to pick up more passengers for New York.

On 10th May 1940, it was still at sea off the English coast when dramatic news was announced by the ship's captain over the shortwave radio that Adolf Hitler had sent his troops over the border into Belgium, Holland and France. Much of Western Europe was now occupied and under Nazi control. The crew of the *SS Pennland* comprised mainly Dutch nationals. An anxious period ensued while the captain waited to see if they would be forced to turn back. The all-clear was finally given to continue the journey to America, but one fear was uppermost in Howard's mind. What about his parents and Margot? Had their ship sailed?

Howard's parents and sister had already left Luxembourg and were en route to the port of Rotterdam for safe passage to America. Because of the Nazi invasion of the Low Countries, they found themselves caught between Holland and Belgium. After almost nine months of freedom, they were once again trapped inside the borders of the Nazi regime.

The *SS Pennland* made the perilous journey across the Atlantic with the risk of U-boat attacks. It finally docked at New York on 15 May. Howard's first feelings on arrival were not so much his impression of the New York skyline or America itself but huge relief at having arrived at all. Crossing the Atlantic was no mean feat in wartime. A journey which usually took four to five days had taken three weeks.

LAND OF LIBERTY

Howard was met at the dock by his father's cousin, Bernie Rau, and wife Hortenfe who had given the original affidavits to the family. They turned out to be a strange couple who took Howard to stay with other relatives in Kew Gardens, Long Island, New York. Eventually, Bernie found a room for Howard in the home of a German-Jewish family, paying the rent on his behalf. Bernie himself lived in a big suite at the Park Lane Hotel, Park Avenue in New York. In the winter, he went off to Miami and in the summer, a few weeks to Colorado Springs. The rest of the year, he lived at the Park Lane Hotel.

During the first fortnight after immigration, Howard did little except stay in his room or spend time with cousins in the same neighbourhood. He then worked for a time for a relative in an import-export business which assembled fountain pens and other items. If he got paid, it was not very much.

Towards the end of June 1940, Howard was to begin a new life in Detroit after his uncle Kurt who had emigrated from Germany in 1935, a survivor of Dachau, drove from Detroit with his wife Ruth to pick him up. They drove the distance of some 800 miles and stayed overnight in a motel. Howard recalls with some humour: 'it was their first wedding anniversary and I cramped their quarters in the motel.'

After spending a few days with Kurt and Ruth at their home in Detroit, Howard rented a room through one of their acquaintances. From there, he was able to visit his aunt and uncle regularly. He found work as an apprentice in a small tool factory.

In those first anxious weeks and months in the United States, there was no news from Howard's parents or sister. The only information he had was the knowledge that Holland had been invaded by German forces. He hoped that his parents had somehow managed to get to England and because of the chaos of war had not been able to contact him. After a time, he began to enquire from other relatives, but no one had any news.

Several weeks later, the first letter from his parents came via friends, the Adlers in Switzerland. Howard learned that his father had already been arrested by the Belgians and then interned in a French camp. His mother was still in Belgium with Margot. Any contact with them was sporadic. That was as much as Howard knew. As he waited for further news, the Japanese carried out a surprise attack on American ships in Pearl Harbour on 7th December 1941. The United States entered the war on the side of Britain. Howard's war would take a new unexpected direction.

CHAPTER FIVE

FIGHTING BACK

WITH AMERICA NOW in the war against Nazi Germany, Howard volunteered to fight in the US forces. In his mind, this was his opportunity to join the battle against the Hitler Regime and play his part in the downfall of Nazism. This was his war and one which he was prepared to fight because the regime had thrown him out of his country and destroyed his family life. He therefore felt no guilt at his decision to join the Allied forces that would eventually see fighting against his former countrymen.

Applying first for the Marine Corps, then the US Navy and American Army, Howard received unexpected rejections because he did not have American citizenship. There was nothing he could do but wait for his call-up papers to come through. In the meantime, he continued working at the factory. Finally in July 1943, at the age of twenty, those papers arrived and he was drafted into the US forces.

Issued with army number 36865227, Howard enlisted into an infantry division in the rank of Private and trained as a machine gunner. The training lasted several months and was extremely intense and demanding. During this period, because of his fluency in German, he tried to volunteer for interpreter duties but all attempts fell on deaf ears.

During the remainder of 1943 and into 1944, American military commanders were making detailed preparations with British commanders for an Allied invasion of Europe. American forces began to leave the United States to be stationed at bases in Britain in readiness for the D-Day landings. In the spring of 1944, having successfully trained as a gunner, Howard was posted overseas with US forces. He boarded a troopship bound for Scotland. It was the second time he had crossed the Atlantic in wartime. He recalls: 'I was a great volunteer and put my name forward for anything going. On board the troopship, I volunteered as a movie projectionist for the army which meant that at least the journey to England was fun.' The troopship docked at Glasgow, from where Howard's unit took a train to Llangollen in North Wales. It was here that the regiment carried out extensive training and final preparations for the invasion.

D-DAY LANDINGS

On 6 June 1944, the flag went up for D-Day – the largest invasion ever mounted by Allied forces. In a single day, the Allies landed 150,000 forces on the beaches of Normandy. The Americans landed on Omaha Beach amidst a horrific 94% rate of casualties and fatalities. Further along the coast at Arromanches, British forces were also landing as part of the massive invasion force. The following day, D-Day+1, Howard's unit crossed the English Channel to Omaha Beach. He said: 'It was a very exciting time but also one full of trepidation. The first landings had taken place and we were in the second wave. We were replacing the troops which had suffered such huge losses the previous day.'

So it was that on 7 June 1944, Howard landed on Omaha Beach with the 86th Replacement Battalion. Casualties were still high and the life expectancy for a machine gunner that day was around 30 seconds. By some miracle, Howard survived the landing and advanced up the beach to take cover in the hedgerows with his unit. How did he keep his nerve under the circumstances? He comments: 'Any soldier who landed on Omaha Beach is always asked the same question. Some were afraid, but most of us did not believe we were about to die. We were young and somehow youth harbours the feeling of invincibility. Even though colleagues were dying on the battlefield around me, you don't think it is going to happen to you.'

The D-Day landings had an unexpected twist of fate for Howard and one that would change his contribution to the war. On the second day of fighting, he picked up a leaflet which appealed for German-speakers to come forward. They were needed in US Military Intelligence, specifically for work at Headquarters. Although the precise nature of the work was not given, Howard assumed it had something to do with typing duties or compiling reports. He had tried for so long to use his knowledge of German for the war effort and now this looked like his chance had come.

'I thought it ironic,' he says, 'because back in the United States I had tried to get into US Intelligence but couldn't. Now on Omaha Beach finally I could.'

Howard showed the leaflet to an officer who was involved in the classification of soldiers in the Replacement Battalion. The officer put his name forward and shortly afterwards he was dispatched to Headquarters. To his surprise, headquarters consisted of a foxhole.

As Allied troops advanced through France that summer and autumn of 1944, Howard remained with the Replacement Battalion for three and a half months. Allied forces crossed the borders into Belgium and Holland and liberated the population. Howard knew that the Allies, including his unit, were ultimately heading for the invasion of Germany. While stationed in Holland, he was pulled out of the battalion and posted to Paris to, ironically, undertake courses in German and intelligence training.

During his time in the French capital, he was acutely concerned about the fate of his parents and sister, last known to have been in Camp Les Milles in the South of France: 'After the liberation of France and Paris, I expected to hear something from my parents. I knew that if they had been liberated somewhere in France, they would have written immediately to our point of contact in Switzerland or to my uncle Kurt in Detroit. I received no news from them at all.'

Snippets of information were already coming through and Howard learned that Jews who were held in Les Milles had been deported to Camp Drancy outside Paris and from there to Auschwitz. By the time Howard was temporarily stationed in Paris, any trace of Camp Drancy had been destroyed by the French authorities. Gaining any further information was difficult. With so much uncertainty surrounding the whereabouts of his family, Howard was posted from Paris back to the theatre of war with the American 5th Corps. His work now kept him fully occupied in the coming months as a member of the Military Intelligence Interpretation team of 5th Corps. He recalls the nature of their work:

> 'Each intelligence team consisted of two officers and four enlisted men. The units worked close to the frontline as American troops pushed towards the Rhine crossings into Germany and then finally Czechoslovakia. As soon as German forces were defeated in a town or village, the military intelligence teams entered and we began our interrogation work of the civilian population. I was part of a team that gathered vital information for US military intelligence. There were times when my unit entered a town before it had been fully liberated and it became very risky work for us. I remained with the Military Intelligence Interpretation team until they reached Pilsen in Czechoslovakia and met Russian troops at the River Elbe.'

LIBERATION OF BUCHENWALD

In April 1945, Howard crossed with his unit into Germany, not as a German refugee this time but an American soldier. It was the first time he had set foot on German soil since he was forced to flee six years earlier. He returned to find much of the country in ruins and the infrastructure destroyed. As preparations were made for his unit to move on, his commanding officer asked to have a word in private.

'I have a really difficult job,' he said to Howard. 'We are going to liberate Buchenwald.'

Howard's mind raced as he asked himself what they would find. There were rumours about the atrocities in the death camps, and he had witnessed firsthand the brutality of Nazism in Munich in the 1930s. Yet, he felt no fear as his army unit was given orders to head into the concentration camp. It was 11th April 1945.

American forces arrived at the gates Buchenwald. The gates were slowly opened and they passed through. Nothing prepared Howard or his comrades for the scale of the horror or the unforgettable stench of rotting corpses piled in their different grotesque positions. He turned his head. The piles of hundreds of children's shoes struck like a dagger through the heart. Emaciated subhuman survivors shuffled around the camp, barely alive, almost unaware of their liberation. Standing amongst the desecration of European Jewry, Howard prayed his parents had not suffered this fate. There had been no news of them since August 1942. As he tried to suppress an involuntary urge to retch, he realized at last that all the personal sacrifices on Omaha Beach were for this moment.

Surrounded by such physical evil, Howard was well aware that he could have been one of these survivors clinging to the last remnants of life. The scenes before him seem momentarily surreal. Here his disdain for the Nazis reached its peak. 'The horror inhabited me and forever I carry the burden of witness,' he said in a documentary made about his life called *Journey to Justice*. He longed for justice to be done; for the perpetrators to be incarcerated in a concentration camp and treated in the same horrific way.

Over the next few days, Howard's unit marched the local German civilian population into the camp to see the atrocities and help remove the corpses. Ordinary Germans suddenly denied any knowledge of the camps or the crimes committed by the regime. Had they turned a blind eye or were they innocent, as claimed? Howard believes they knew what was going on but chose to be bystanders to the Nazi killing machine. Dissent was also muted by fear.

When their macabre duties at Buchenwald were over, Howard's unit crossed into Czechoslovakia on its way to Pilsen, not far from Theresienstadt. He had just received news that his next posting though was to be Nuremberg in Bavaria. He had heard that the most important trial in the history of international justice was about to convene there. Surviving leaders of the Nazi government were to be held accountable for their crimes against humanity and the world. But occupied with intelligence duties on the frontline, Nuremberg meant very little to Howard at that point. To him it was just another place where some Nazis were going to be put on trial. The full reality wouldn't sink in until his arrival at the prison.

THE SEARCH FOR SURVIVORS

Before Nuremberg, Howard had three unfinished tasks: to find his parents, make enquiries about relatives whom he suspected had been deported to Theresienstadt and visit his sister Margot whom he now knew had survived and was living with the Adlers in Zurich.

While in Pilsen, Howard discovered that a Czech intelligence officer was about to bring Czech survivors out of the camp at Theresienstadt. He handed the officer a list of relatives whom he suspected had been transported there in 1942. Two days later, he received a message from one of the guards at the gates of the American military compound. An elderly woman was asking for him.

Howard left his temporary office and crossed the compound. The skeletal, but unmistakable figure, of his seventy year old grandmother, Rosa, stood at the gates. The Czech intelligence officer had discovered her in the camp and brought her to the American compound.

During her three year incarceration in Theresienstadt, Rosa had lost 60 lbs. Howard says today that he will never forget the haunted look in her eyes as he approached her. Yet, he has trouble recalling the rest of that first meeting after so many years of separation. What he does recall is that he brought her into the army camp and gave her the officer's guest room for the night. Then he swiftly found lodgings for her with a local family until he could personally drive her home to Munich, the city she had been taken from by the Nazis in 1942.

On 7 May 1945, Germany signed an unconditional surrender. War was over, but the peace had yet to be won. As Allied forces swept across Germany, the most wanted Nazi war criminals went into hiding and assumed false identities and disguises. The main priority for the Allies was to capture them alive and bring them to trial. Adolf

Hitler was said to have committed suicide with his new wife Eva Braun in his bunker on 30 April, escaping any accountability for his evil and murderous regime. The irony of Howard's own survival and Hitler's death was not lost on him:

> 'Now Hitler was dead; I was still alive. It was a great feeling of triumph which was soon tempered by the discovery of the full extent of what the Nazis had done to Jews in concentration camps and to my own family. I had seen something of this when we liberated Buchenwald, but the world was beginning to learn the full horror.'

Hitler's propaganda minister, Joseph Goebbels, and wife committed suicide the day after Adolf Hitler and Eva Braun. Now the remaining echelons of Nazi government were on the run – fleeing from justice. Concentration camp guards and perpetrators of crimes against humanity were also in hiding, though some successfully fled the country in coming months via the "Odessa" escape network to South America and beyond. Capturing them and bringing them to justice was to prove one of the greatest challenges facing the Allied forces.

It was widely anticipated that Allied success in the denazification process hinged on bringing named war criminals to justice. Teams of ex-German refugees like Howard, now serving in the Allied forces, were sent out to scour the countryside for high-ranking Nazi war criminals whose names were on the 'most wanted' list. There was some measure of success, although in some cases it would take up to a year to investigate, track down the last known movements of a war criminal and find their secret location. Their fluency in German meant they were ideal for this undercover work. Himmler, for example, was finally eventually arrested and brought to Fallingbostel camp where he committed suicide by taking a cyanide pill whilst in British custody.

RETURN TO MUNICH

With Germany's unconditional surrender a satisfying reality, Howard took a jeep to Munich. Beside him, his grandmother in an overcoat with the stripes of a US Lieutenant, given to her by Howard to enable her to pass unchecked through the American zone of Allied-occupied Germany. In a moving gesture, she was saluted by military personnel all the way into Munich. As Howard drove along the potholed highway towards the centre of Munich, the once vibrant city, the birthplace and capital of Nazism, was a wasteland. Ninety per cent lay in ruins; the destruction almost absolute. Howard bore no guilt or pity for the suffering of the German people. He had seen Buchenwald.

With satisfaction, his eyes scanned the once familiar landscape, now an endless pile of rubble and bombed-out buildings. This was a biblical Apocalypse, an appropriate retribution for Nazi crimes against humanity. The local people stared with bewildered faces, stopping momentarily from scavenging the ruins in search of remnants of their belongings. How did they feel about the occupying forces?

As Howard drove on with his skeletal grandmother quietly sat beside him, he was acutely conscious that this was the city of his birth and the place where he grew up. An eon away he had lived a sheltered happy childhood until the Nazis shattered the lives of his family and forced them into poverty. The streets of Munich breathed the memories of extremes. The knock on the door from a woman, merely delivering bread, echoed the frantic bang of the Gestapo and SS men searching for Jewish males after Kristallnacht.

Howard finally pulled up outside 53 Reitmorstrasse, his childhood home for fifteen years. The apartment had suffered minor damage from Allied bombing and was now occupied by non-Jewish Germans who looked with curiosity, part fear, at the American sergeant standing in the doorway. Howard enquired after his parents but they shook their heads in ignorance. He politely said goodbye and turned back to his grandmother waiting in the jeep. He noticed two former neighbours walking down the street towards the jeep. They recognized him immediately in spite of his American army uniform.

A little awkward at first, they were quick to ask about his well-being and other family members. Did they even give him a second thought during the war? News of the atrocities in the concentration camps had already broken to the German nation. They realized their error. Howard noticed a flash of awareness cross their faces that his parents have probably suffered the same fate as the rest of Munich's Jews. Very quickly they were at pains to excuse the situation and said that they were not Nazis. They had no choice but to follow the political flow.

As Howard stood in the ruins of the Third Reich, he realized that the German people were already re-writing history. All of a sudden Germany had no Nazis. No one knew about war crimes, even less had anything to do with them. After a few more words, with accepting grace Howard bad farewell to his former neighbours and climbed back in to the jeep. Giving his grandmother a reassuring smile, he started the engine and headed for the place where she was going to live until new permanent accommodation could be found for her.

Then with his grandmother finally settled, Howard left for Switzerland on a week's compassionate leave.

CHAPTER SIX

DEAR TREASURE,

I T WAS FIVE years since Howard had seen his sister, Margot. He had said goodbye to an eleven year old girl on a station platform in Luxembourg in 1940. Now Margot was sixteen and about to enter womanhood. Howard learnt that she had survived and was lodging with the Adlers in Zurich, the family intermediary in Switzerland who had sent money from relatives in America. The Adlers had been their lifeline during the war. Unlike the last goodbye, the reunion with Margot was an emotional one. Decades later, Margot is still tearful when she recalls their reunion. For her, it was a moment of pride too to see her brother in American army uniform and yet pain that she had to tell him about their parents. Margot's wartime experience was a very different story…

On 9th May 1940, Berthold, Lina and Margot had left Diekirch in Luxembourg for Holland. They were due to sail from Rotterdam to America the following day and overnight they stayed in a hotel in Antwerp. During that night, they were woken by intense bombing and gunfire. In the confusion, no one in the area knew what was happening. They rose very early the next morning and took a bus to Rotterdam. They soon discovered that German forces had moved at an alarming rate into the Low Countries and occupied them. It was 10th May 1940. The bus did not make it to the port of Rotterdam, only as far as Rosendahl, near the Dutch-Belgian border.

Margot recounted how they had then walked for five hours before being arrested by Dutch police. Their arrest by Dutch police was not because they were Jews but because they were Germans and therefore of enemy nationality. Holland was technically at war with Germany so the Triests were now 'the enemy' and no longer treated as refugees fleeing Nazi oppression. Margot recalls:

> 'We were herded into a truck with others who had been arrested. As we passed through the small town of Rosendahl, the whole town went up in flames. We just missed the bombs falling behind us. We were taken to an old Armoury where the men were separated from the women and children. The tribunal decided that we were Jewish, not German, and could therefore be released.'

The Triests were eventually released from detention, but they had nowhere to go. They were once again trapped again inside Nazi-occupied Europe. Luftwaffe planes droned overhead, parachuting German soldiers into Holland and Belgium. Nothing could prevent the total German occupation.

CAMP LES MILLES

With chaos all around them Berthold took Lina and Margot across the border into Belgium. But Berthold's freedom was short lived. He was arrested and would never taste freedom again. Taken first to Camp Gurs in France, he was then transferred to Camp Les Milles, a disused brick factory at Les Milles near Marseilles. There at the factory, hundreds of Europe's Jewish intellectuals and artists were being held. Conditions were bare, with no water, sanitation or heating throughout the winter months. Internees slept on the hard floor on the second level of a disused building.

After Berthold's arrest, Lina and Margot remained in Belgium. Lina was determined to see her husband again. With money she had cashed in from an insurance policy and hidden in their belongings, she purchased fake identity papers to take them into France. In an act of betrayal, the man who sold her the forged documents was working for both sides and denounced them to the authorities during their journey to Marseilles. For six months, Lina and Margot endured harsh conditions in a French prison before being unexpectedly released on condition they return to Brussels. Ever resourceful and determined not to desert her husband, Lina decided to make her way with Margot to Marseilles. For nearly another six months, they were able to live in freedom and rent a small room in Marseilles.

At that time, it was possible for internees to apply for weekend release from Camp Les Milles, the only condition that they report back on Sunday evening and not attempt to escape. Berthold was granted leave over several weekends to spend time with Lina and Margot. These were precious moments in such unstable and terrifying times for Europe's Jews. The Triests settled into this routine for the next year, perhaps little suspecting that their lives would be threatened.

THE ROUND-UP OF THE JEWS

One fateful day in the second week of January 1942, the Vichy Government as collaborators of the Nazis, rounded up all foreign Jews living in the region. Vichy police officers came to arrest Lina and Margot. Given just half an hour to pack their belongings, they were escorted to Camp Les Milles. Now they joined Berthold and nearly two thousand other Jews crammed in the camp. For the young Margot, it was a terrifying time. Her fears surfaced in a nightmare dream one night when she imagined that she was separated from her parents who were killed by the Nazis. Her mother, ever strong and reassuring, comforted her and told her it was only a dream.

The nightmare became reality just days later when members of the French organisation OSE visited Les Milles camp and explained that parents were being given a choice by the authorities of handing over their children to the relief organisation or remaining together in the camp. Either option was risky, but the charity workers implored parents to let their children go and not face the deportations by train which they knew would surely happen soon. The OSE (Organisation to Save the Children) was already working hard to smuggle Jewish children out of Vichy France to the safety of neutral countries. Some were hidden in children's homes in the French countryside, aided by the French Resistance Movement.

Berthold and Lina made the painful decision to send Margot with the OSE. They felt it would give her more chance of survival. Little did they know then, but only a short time later, parents were no longer given this option by the authorities and Jewish children perished in the death camps alongside their parents.

The pain of separation was too much for Berthold and he broke down. Lina assured her daughter that they would see her again soon. Deep down, and even though she was only eleven, Margot instinctively knew it was the end. She comments: 'My mother showed no fear when we parted. She was a very strong woman.'

Margot was escorted with other Jewish children to waiting buses outside the camp gates. The pain and scars of that day run deep and continue to haunt her over seventy years later.

The OSE took the children to a safe-house in Marseilles for a few days. Lina Triest were given the address. In the desperate hours before Lina and Berthold's fate was sealed, and fearing the worst was about to befall them, Lina penned a postcard to Margot in Marseilles and a letter to the Adlers in Switzerland. She kept them safe in her pocket for the day she could post them herself.

On 12 August 1942, the two and a half thousand Jews in Camp Les Milles were rounded-up into groups and herded outside the camp gates to waiting trains. As they climbed into the carriages, with a final glance back at the brick factory, Berthold and Lina were in no doubt about their fate. They were about to be deported to an unknown destination.

Finally, as the freight train sped through the French countryside with its human cargo, and thinking only of her children, Lina slipped the postcard and letter through a tiny crack in a small open window. She had no idea if either would reach their destinations.

Whoever found them at the side of the railway line, perhaps a farmer or someone walking their dog, probably did not suspect the terrible circumstances surrounding them. They picked them up and posted them. Eventually the letter reached the Adlers in Switzerland, and Margot received the postcard in Marseilles a few days later. The last words of her mother were heart wrenching because Lina knew she would never see her daughter again:

> Little Treasure,
> I am so glad you arrived well. I am sure you have found girlfriends already. Take care of yourself, little one. Always be well and have fun. I will write as often as I can and you my dear child should do the same. Always be my brave little girl and with God's help, we will see each other again. I send you many thousand kisses.
> Your Mummy.

The Jewish children rescued by the OSE were not safe to remain in Marseilles for any length of time. Every few days, they were moved to other safe-houses in remote parts of France. Margot and around a hundred children were taken to a large country estate, Chateau du Couret, near Limoges in the mountains of Eastern France. There they lived in hiding for four months until the Gestapo began intensifying their search for Jewish children.

The OSE decided to move them again, this time across the border into the safety of Switzerland. Margot and the girls were transferred to a secret boarding house in the border town of Annemasse where they spent the first night. Margot was informed that very soon she would be given a group of ten young girls from the age of four to escort over the border in the middle of the night. The route – a remote part of the railway track into Switzerland.

WALK TO FREEDOM

The 19th April 1943 was Margot's fourteenth birthday and one that she would never forget. That night, she led ten young girls along the railway track towards freedom. Leading from the front, she implored them to keep quiet and not crunch on the gravel between the sleepers so no one from nearby houses betrayed them to Nazi patrols. 'The children were petrified,' she says today. 'I had to calm their fears and not show my own fear.'

The walk to freedom took twenty long minutes. But soon they crossed into Switzerland and were safe. They were the lucky one who had escaped the clutches of the Nazis. Margot travelled on to the Adlers in Zurich where she stayed for the rest of the war.

Talking with Howard after being reunited in 1945, it was clear that Margot was emotionally traumatized by her experiences in Belgium and France. As Howard listened, she suddenly reached into her pocket and pulled out an envelope. Tears welled in her eyes as she passed it to him.

Howard glanced down and saw his mother's neatly formed handwriting.

The envelope was postmarked Nimes, the date 13 August 1942, and addressed to the Adlers. The letter had made it all the way from Vichy France to Switzerland. Because of the censorship of mail by the Vichy government, Lina knew that she had to be careful about names contained in the letter, so she often substituted family names for pet-names. In some places, she used real names. Noticeably, she gave Margot several different names to protect her identity because Margot was in hiding somewhere in France at the time the letter was written.

Where coded names were used, Howard today has added the real names in brackets. From the reference in the letter to their friends travelling 'farther than Rosa' (the grandmother in Theresienstadt), it is clear that Lina and Berthold knew where they were heading. It was the last letter Lina ever wrote:

My dear friends,

I want to confirm your dear letter of the 5th because I don't know whether it will still be possible tomorrow. Did you receive Lisa's [Lina] telegram and card? What do you say about this bad luck? We are quite desperate. Please leave Kurt's message with Edith [Adler] until you have a new address. Margot had to separate from her parents. The goodbye was terrible but could not be changed. Dodolein [Margot] is presently in a children's home of the OSE... Poor Heinzl [Howard] will be sad and worried because he does not receive any mail from his parents. I am already with my husband the past 8 days [in Camp Les Milles]; Ellen too was here [Margot]. Many of our friends have already left. I believe they travelled farther than Rosa [Howard's grandmother in Theresienstadt]. The fact that I have had no news from mother [Rosa] is very depressing… The long trip will be very strenuous for Paps [Howard's father] and Heddy's sister [herself] is quite afraid… I will close now. If possible I will always write to you and please try to do the same. And please stay in touch with the children [Howard & Margot].

I always feel that I should awake from a deep sleep. Thank you again for all your love. Our intimate greetings your Ly T. and Berthold.'

PART 3

NUREMBERG PRISON

Chapter Seven

LIFE BEHIND BARS

WITH THE KNOWLEDGE of the contents of his mother's last letter, Sergeant Howard Triest arrived at Nuremberg Prison on 25 September 1945. For him, there was no sense that he was about to witness history in the making or that the Nuremberg Trials would become one of the most defining moments of history. For this euphoric twenty-two year old American soldier arriving as part of the Allied forces, Nuremberg was significant only for the present. It represented justice for millions of victims including himself who had suffered at the hands of the Nazis. By the time he arrived there, he had lost any trace of a German accent. Little did he know that he was about to make his most important contribution to the American forces and one where his original German background would prove essential.

The imposing red-brick three-storey building which housed the prison and courtroom was to be the focus of international justice for twelve months. The heavy security presence and armoured vehicles surrounding the prison meant the Allies were taking no chances with those detained behind its bars. It also served as a stark warning to Nuremburg's population eking out an existence in the bombed-out city that a new era of occupation had dawned for the sins the German people had allowed their leaders to commit. Incarcerated in the cells were the twenty-two surviving leaders of the former Nazi government awaiting trial for crimes against humanity on an unprecedented scale and horror.

As Howard checked in with the security guards, he suddenly felt a growing sense that justice may now be done. Although he had no idea of his previse role there, he was to head for the office of the American Commandant of the prison, situated in the main building behind the courthouse, separate from the buildings which housed the jail cells. Colonel Burton Andrus was not only the commandant, but head of 6850th Internal Security Detachment under the International Military Tribunal, in charge of the defendants at the jail. Howard was about to join Andrus's team.

COLONEL ANDRUS

Howard vividly remembers his first day at Nuremberg – of knocking on the door of Andrus's office and entering to find the 53-year old Colonel sitting at his desk engrossed in paperwork.

'Reporting for duty, Colonel,' said Howard, standing to attention in his dark green army uniform.

Through black round-rimmed glasses, Andrus made penetrating eye contact. 'Good day Sergeant Triest,' he said. 'I will waste no time in getting to the point. You are here to act as interpreter to the American psychiatrist, Dr Kelley, who is working with the defendants. As a fluent German speaker and bi-lingual, your role is to accompany him into the cells on a daily basis. This will surely be your most important contribution to the American forces so far.'

Howard concealed any reaction to Andrus's last comment. Granted that he hoped justice would be done, but how could the work in the prison be more important than landing with troops on Omaha Beach? Than defeating Nazi Germany?

Before dismissing him, Andrus added a warning: 'This is a tight establishment, Sergeant. There is to be no fraternization with the defendants. They are criminals, not prisoners of war.'

Howard left the office with a lump in his throat. It suddenly dawned on him that he would be coming face-to-face with Hitler's former leaders: Julius Streicher, the biggest Jew-baiter in the Nazi regime; Rudolf Hess, Hitler's one-time deputy who walked the fine curb between sanity and madness, and Hermann Goering whose exalted self-importance and flamboyant extravagance defined him as the most arrogant of them all. Howard knew that few people would come so physically close to the men who once ran Nazi Germany. Now Howard would be able to assess for himself. Were they different from other men? How would they react to a German-Jewish refugee coming into their cell? In answer to the latter, they would never know. Howard's past would never be revealed. It would remain a closely guarded secret and something respected by the other prison staff.

Howard was there to do a job and could not let the blind prejudice of the defendants interfere with the process. This silence about his past was to have the most

unexpected outcome. The subject of whom or what constituted a Jew or a German would ironically be played out in
front of Howard by the defendants and lead to an unfore-
seen question of trust, particularly with Julius Streicher.

THE PSYCHIATRISTS

Leaving Colonel Andrus's office, Howard headed straight
for Dr Kelley's office. Kelley shared a large office with
American psychologist Dr Gustav Gilbert who was there
to carry out his own analysis of the defendants. Gilbert
largely kept himself to himself and rarely socialized with
Howard or Dr Kelley. Able to speak fluent German,
Gilbert conducted his own interviews in the cells and kept
copious notes from the very beginning with the express
aim of writing a book after the trial. His extensive diary
has been published as *Nuremberg Diary*. Gilbert, Kelley
and Howard were in a unique position in that they were
issued with special security passes enabling them access
to the prison twenty-four hours a day, seven days a week.

Howard and Kelley's job was made easier because
the strict solitary conditions at Mondorf in Luxembourg,
codenamed "Ashcan", where all the defendants, except
Speer and Schacht, had been held for three months before
Nuremberg, meant that the defendants had rarely com-
municated with anyone.

'Consequently,' comments Howard, 'when the defendants arrived at Nuremberg they were only too ready to
talk to us.'

There was no question in anyone's mind of the importance of Kelley and Howard's work. The psychiatric team

at Nuremberg was there to observe the defendants on a daily basis, to ensure they were mentally fit to stand trial and not about to commit suicide. The last thing the legal teams wanted was to have their power to execute justice thwarted by a suicide or a diagnosis of insanity.

Perhaps surprisingly, it was not Howard or Kelley's job to take down evidence of atrocities from the former leaders of the Nazi Regime. Their role was ask particular questions and record the responses to seek an answer to the question on everyone's mind: why are these men so different from ordinary people and able to give orders to kill millions of people?

'In the end,' says Howard, 'I'm not sure we found an adequate response or that these questions were ever really answered. All too often the pitiful defendants ranted for hours about the defeat of Hitler and how Germany had lost the war. None admitted guilt or showed any remorse, with the possible exception of Hans Frank.

But how would Howard, a former German-Jewish refugee, react to being so close to the perpetrators of such horrendous crimes? Crimes which he himself had witnessed in Buchenwald? To those who had effectively signed the death warrants for his parents? These questions will be answered as the story of his time in Nuremberg unfolds.

In spite of Colonel Andrus's warning that the accused were to be treated as war criminals, an unprompted 'rapport' developed with some of them and one with the most unexpected outcome. Not heeding Andrus's words, psychiatrist Dr Kelley treated the defendants professionally – as patients rather than war criminals. This kind of interaction was bound to change Howard and Kelley's experience of Nuremberg. Howard's story now moves into extraordinary terrain and the heart of his experience at Nuremberg. In no time at all, Howard and Kelley began to walk a tightrope between professional distance and fraternization. Did they befriend the defendants? Howard is absolutely clear that they did not. Did the defendants befriend them? In some cases, most definitely yes.

As a result, Howard would later leave Nuremberg with 22 books signed by the defendants, each with a personal inscription. The most anti-Semitic of them all, Julius Streicher, saw Howard as an ally because, with Howard's blond hair and blue eyes, Streicher thought him a true Aryan. In his blind prejudice, Streicher trusted Howard and frequently referred to him as his 'my Aryan friend', even to the other staff. It was always going to be a one-way relationship though. Ironically, Streicher died on the gallows giving the Hitler salute, never knowing that his 'Aryan friend' was a German Jew whom he would have willingly exterminated during the Final Solution.

Initially, Howard speaks only in very broad general terms about his work in the jail; about how he and Kelley spent up to eight hours a day interviewing the defendants, frequently well into the evening. He speaks about how they spent more time, day and night, with the defendants than any of the judges or Defense Counsel in the court itself. They allowed the defendants to ramble on at leisure which resulted in them being told things matters which did not necessarily relate to the prisoners' political actions or crimes. They learnt about the prisoners' basic human anxieties.

Kelley always believed it was important to gauge the defendants' reactions to certain happenings in the court and try to understand what made them tick. Nothing the defendants ever said in the cells made any difference to the outcome of the trial. The legal procedures were all based on their record before they were captured. The judges had to work strictly on the documentary evidence alongside statements by both Counsel and testimony from witnesses.

Kelley's brief was not to interrogate the defendants or seek confessions, but to understand what their motives had been in running the Third Reich and how they could have committed such horrendous atrocities. Howard recalls: 'Kelley told me that we were there to see if we could dissect pure evil.' Kelley summarized the work in his book, *22 Cells in Nuremberg*:

> 'As a scientist, I regarded my duty in the jail to be not only to guard the health of men facing trial for war crimes but also to study them as a researcher in a laboratory… I took it upon myself to examine the personality patterns of these men and, to a degree, the techniques they employed to win and hold power.'

Through Howard as translator, Kelley asked his questions of the defendants and received their answers. Nothing was confrontational. These were strictly interviews where the prisoners talked about what was on their mind, which gave them an opportunity to pour out their hearts. On occasion, they mentioned mundane matters, like the food in the prison or how they were missing their families. From time to time, they were very open about the pain of not seeing their families. 'It certainly affected them as it would most human beings,' comments Howard. 'We sometimes expect war criminals to be immune from ordinary emotions because of the nature of their crimes, but that was not the case.'

ENCOUNTERING THE ACCUSED

Over seven decades later, Howard talks in a relaxed, though detached way, about his encounter with the accused. The weight of evidence against them was so insurmountable as to make their guilt indisputable, and yet, as he discovered within days of arriving in the prison that (with the possible exception of Hans Frank) none of them saw themselves guilty of any evil. It was the predominant theme running through what they told him every day. They resolutely clung to their anti-Semitic ideology and showed no remorse for their crimes. In his soft accent which is hard to place, neither German nor American, Howard explains:

'All of a sudden we didn't have bad people in the prison cells. They believed they were doing good things for Germany! They saw themselves as innocent of any wrong-doing. Hans Frank was the only one who became very religious and showed us some remorse. It is one thing to show remorse later in the prison cell when you know it's a matter of going to the gallows but we never knew if it was all show or genuine feeling.'

Many months of interesting work lay ahead, but it was an emotionally draining time. Howard entered the cells of all former members of the Nazi government and spent significant periods of time with them. The sense of euphoria at the Allied victory was often tempered by the knowledge that he was as close as anyone could be to those who had committed unprecedented evil against humanity, including his own family. Remaining calm and emotionally detached when conversing with the defendants would be a constant challenge. Being shrewd enough not to mention his Jewish background, he and Kelley secured more out of them. Howard's civility towards the defendants served a singular purpose and enabled him to carry out his job effectively.

In spite of being given his mother's last letter by Margot, there was still no definite proof that their parents were dead. Howard did not give up the search, even though deep down he suspected the terrible truth. He clung to the unrealistic hope that somehow they might have escaped, be suffering from amnesia and living back in Munich. He lived this paradox for the whole year that he was in the Nuremberg Prison.

In the coming months, Howard paid several visits to the city of his birth, only two and a half hours drive from Nuremberg. Saving up his army pay, he purchased an old American army jeep to drive regularly to Munich to visit his surviving grandmother and continue the search for his parents. By this time, most concentration camp survivors and those in Displaced Person Camps had made contact with their relatives even if they had not yet returned home. There had been no such news from Lina or Berthold

Triest. Howard's hopes were unrealistic, but a necessary part of his own psychological survival.

A VERY PERSONAL JOB

In late November 1945, Howard's papers came through to be demobbed from American forces and sent back to the United States. Before his shift duty one morning, Colonel Andrus called him into his office. Andrus looked at him with the same steely gaze as the first day Howard had arrived at Nuremberg two months earlier.

'I know you are about to be demobbed, but I need you to stay on as interpreter to Kelley,' he said, unsure of Howard's response. Andrus understood the difficulty given his original background. He cleared his throat and continued: 'Would you be willing to continue your work here, but in a civilian capacity? It is a just formality on paper but if you agree, you are needed until the end of the trial.'

Howard needed no time to think over the proposal. 'Yes sir. I would be pleased to serve further under your command.'

'Good, then that is decided,' said Andrus.

What was Howard's motivation for agreeing to Andrus's request? It was a sense that not many personnel would come as close to the defendants as Howard and the psychiatrists. The trial was only a few weeks in. 'It was a feeling of needing to see this through to its conclusion,' he says in a measured way.

'Having been so closely tied to prison life, I realized that this was an opportunity that was part of history in the making. I knew that. And I could be part of it. There was something fascinating, albeit difficult, but compelling about the work. But more than that, I wanted to see justice done. I felt a sense of duty to do what I could, however small, in the process of ensuring these men paid for their crimes.'

Having agreed to stay on, he could not foresee the extraordinary rapport that would emerge between him and the defendants in the coming months. He recounts again, with a hint of amusement: 'I found myself in an unusual situation because my original Jewish background was never discovered by any of the defendants and in some cases I became their trusted American friend.'

The formalities of the discharge and reengagement as a civilian needed to be carried out. Howard travelled to the city of Bamberg, the birthplace of his father, not far from Nuremberg. It was there on 6th November 1945 he was formally discharged from the US forces. In a twist of fate, he found himself demobbed in the same army barracks as his father had been inducted into the German army in the First World War. In the garrison that day, it was a time for reflection. Howard remembered how proud his father had been to fight for Germany, how his father had shown him photographs of himself in German uniform and talked about the Iron Cross he had been awarded for bravery. Howard reflects: 'my father loved Germany. It was his homeland until the Nazis forced him and our family out.'

Reporting back to Andrus at the prison, Howard was re-assigned to the War Department as a civilian employee with officer status equivalent to Captain. Now instead of wearing a uniform with officer's insignia, his officer's clothing had sewn onto each jacket lapel a small triangle cloth patch with the letters "US" in the middle. Since civilian army protocol prevented him from living in army barracks, Andrus instructed him to find a suitable apartment in the city and requisition it for special use. Howard carried out his instructions and found a district on the outskirts of Nuremberg that had not suffered such heavy bombing. There, he shared an apartment with another American colleague, Britt Bailey, who was also working in the prison. They became good friends. Transport to the prison was provided every day by the motor-pool of the courthouse and, although Howard was permitted to wear civilian clothes, he chose not to because in enemy country it was still not advisable. For lunch meals he, Britt and other prison staff took a ten minute walk from the prison complex to the Grand Hotel where many dignitaries connected to the trial were staying. Work with Dr Kelley continued exactly as it had before, however, it would prove impossible to remain unaffected by the personal contact with the accused.

THE BOOK SIGNINGS

In the autumn of 1945, Howard accompanied Dr Kelley on brief business to the small town of Erlangen, not far from Nuremberg. While Howard no longer remembers the reason for their trip, one memory stands out. Here, they visited the university library and found all Nazi books had been confiscated by the Allied occupying forces as part of the denazification process. Amongst the piles of books waiting to be removed, Howard noticed some written by the key defendants being held at Nuremberg.

In that moment, he had an idea to take copies back to the prison and get the defendants to sign them. He pulled out relevant books and made his own pile. It included a special leather-bound, gold-edged Edition of *Mein Kampf* printed in 1939 to mark Hitler's 50th birthday. Inside was stamped with a copy of Hitler's signature. He loaded them all into the army truck and took them back to Nuremberg. Howard eventually returned to the United States in 1947 with twenty-two books signed at Nuremberg, twenty-one of them by the main defendants; the last signed by eight Field Marshals and Generals.

The saga of the book-signings was extraordinary. Some inscriptions read like a message to an acquaintance rather than the enemy who was also essentially the victor. Surely these fallen men, on trial for their lives, felt some resentment towards their American captors and guards in the prison, including Howard? None of that is reflected in what they wrote to him. He says:

> 'They sat behind bars, humiliated, defeated men, their country in ruins and devastated by Allied armies, their lives about to be crushed under the weight of justice. And yet they could still strike an amicable and polite accord with me. It had, perhaps, to do with the inter-personal relationship which had inadvertently developed between myself and the accused.'

In January 1946, Walther Funk signed to Howard inside a copy of *Ein Leben fuer die Wirtschaft*: 'In memory of the Nuremberg prison time. Jan '46 Walther Funk.' The personalised inscription links the point at which Howard's life crosses Funk's, almost naturally as if he was inscribing a holiday greeting or postcard. Funk viewed it as a souvenir of their time in the prison.

On 3 February 1946, Howard went into Hans Fritzsche's cell clutching a copy of *Angriff, Angriff*. In it Fritzsche penned a lengthier inscription in German and one which firmly suggested that the guilt was not all on Germany's side. In translation it reads: 'that was the clean beginning, then came an honest battle, on the end there was a crime. Unfortunately the guilt does not lie on one side. Hans Fritzsche, 3 Feb '46.'

The next defendant, Wilhelm Frick, had gained a level of cordial trust in Howard such that he wrote inside the book *Wir bauen das Dritte Reich*: 'Mr Triest, in friendly memory, Frick 3.2.46'. Howard was by now a familiar face in the cell and Frick bore no ill-feeling towards the American interpreter standing in front of him. He might have felt differently had he known Howard's Jewish background.

Albert Speer, Hitler's Minister for Armaments, was one of the least intimidating figures. In his cell, Speer passed a copy of *Deutsche Kuenstler Unserer Zeit* to Howard and signed to 'Mr Triest, in memory of the time in the Nuremberg prison, Albert Speer, 3.2.46.'

The basic inscriptions given by the next four defendants perhaps highlight the fact that they remained much more aloof towards him than the weightier figures of Goering and Streicher. Inside *Die Hitlerjugend*, von Schirach simply signed: 'To Mr Triest, Baldur von Schirach,

3.2.46.' Schacht, former president of the Reichsbank and government minister from 1939-1943, wrote similarly: 'To Mr Howard Triest, Hjalmar Schacht, 4.2.46.' Alfred Rosenberg kept his inscription brief and simple. In *Der Sumpf*, he wrote: 'A Rosenberg, Nuremberg 3.2.46.' And von Neurath in *Stresemann*: 'In memory of the year 1946, L. Freiherr von Neurath'.

The final signature obtained at this time was that of Franz von Papen. Howard found him still to be the slick diplomat who certainly felt he should not be in Nuremberg. His belief that he should not be indicted as a war criminal is reflected in the ironic sentence which he wrote to Howard in a copy of *Appell an das Deutsche Gewissen*: 'In memory of a criminal, Nuremberg Feb 1946, Franz von Papen.' As he handed the book back to Howard, von Papen scoffed at the very thought he was a war criminal.

Former Foreign Minister von Ribbentrop's personalised inscription inside the book *Der Freiheitfampf Europas* was cordial and surprisingly upbeat: 'To Mr Howard Triest wishing all good luck, Joachim von Ribbentrop, Nuremberg 1946.' Inscriptions from defendants Kaltenbrunner and Seyss-Inquart were written a couple of months later in May and June respectively. Again, their dedications were basic, a possible indication again of the aloofness between them and Howard. Inside *SS Leitheft*, Kaltenbrunner signed: 'Kaltenbrunner, 24.5.46.' Inside *Hitler in seiner Heimat*, Seyss-Inquart wrote: 'Seyss-Inquart, Nuremberg, 22.6.46.'

What were Howard's motivations behind these inscriptions? He replies: 'as a souvenir of my time at

Nuremberg and tangible reminder of a difficult personal period. It was a unique collection that provided a physical anchor for my memories of Nuremberg. It was something I could show my friends and family when I returned to America to say that I really had been there. I had been with the leaders who had killed my people. For me it was about remembrance – remembrance of Nuremberg. I never thought back then that the trial would attract the interest and have the status that it does today.'

DR GOLDENSOHN

In January 1946, Kelly left Nuremberg and returned to the United States. In his autobiography *22 Cells in Nuremberg*, Kelley wrote that Goering, ever the dramatist, 'wept unashamedly' when he [Kelley] left for America. On 8 January 1946, the thirty-four year old psychiatrist Dr Leon Goldensohn arrived to replace him. Howard worked well with both psychiatrists, but found Goldensohn's temperament different from Kelley. He says, 'Goldensohn was not prone to periods of moodiness like Kelley. Because I worked longer with Goldensohn, we became friends.'

Colonel Andrus briefed Goldensohn on the twenty-one surviving defendants being held in the prison. Goldensohn would soon be able to make his own analysis of them. Even now, the defendants were still obsessed with explaining Hitler's defeat, why Germany had been razed to the ground and Nazism crushed. A nation that had been brainwashed for twelve years with Nazi ideology found it difficult to adjust to failure. Much of the interviews were taken up with the defendants trying to explain and justify

Germany's defeat. Howard and Goldensohn listened to their lengthy explanations, but nothing could change their fate. That was in the hands of the courtroom.

Over the course of nine months, the psychiatrists carried out various psychological tests and an IQ assessment of the defendants. This included use of the Rorschach Ink Blot Test. Invented by Swiss psychiatrist Hermann Rorschach in 1921 and used widely in America, the test comprised ten cards each with an enlarged ink blot on them. Five cards were black and white, two black and red, and the three other various colours. The defendants were shown a series of cards of different colour ink blots, always in the same sequence. Depending on what they saw in the cards formed the basis of the psychiatrist's analysis.

Kelley and Goldensohn both concluded that, with the exception of Rudolf Hess and probably Hans Frank, the defendants were not mentally ill. All, apart from Julius Streicher, were found to be above average intelligence. That made it even harder to understand the atrocities which they had committed and to analyse 'pure' evil. The same question kept going over in the minds of Howard and the psychiatrists: how could men of such intelligence commit crimes of mass murder? No satisfactory answer was ever reached.

BUCHENWALD REVISITED

Because of his position in the prison, Howard was able to secure a privileged pass for the Press section to attend certain sessions of the trial. Being with the Press gave him a prime view of everything that was going on:

'It was an historic sight. Having been used to seeing the defendants in their cells on their own, the courtroom gave a chance to see them altogether. They looked like a Motley crew. The irony was not lost on me that here in front of a court of international justice sat the most powerful men in Germany who had once run the country of my birth. It was a tremendous feeling of relief when the trial got started because now I could feel that the world was on the road to justice.'

There were days that were monotonous even in this trial. During the early weeks, Howard chose to attend for a couple of hours at a time. He found much of the time taken up with argument of detailed points of law. The defendants often looked bored. One particular day interested Howard more than the others. The 13 December was the day evidence of crimes at Buchenwald was going to be shown. Howard entered the press box and sat down.

The prosecution brought in a collection of shrunken human heads as exhibits – these had come from Buchenwald, collected by Ilse Koch, the wife of the camp commandant. She had earned the nickname the 'Witch of Buchenwald'. Her brutality was particularly shocking and unexpected because she was a woman. Her husband proved to be equally brutal.

Ilse Koch delighted in using the shrunken heads of prisoners, mainly Jews, as statues in her office and home. She had also organized the use of tattooed human skin for lampshades. Howard heard the gasps of horror and felt the sense of shock amongst members of the press around him. For him, this evidence was not a shock because he had entered Buchenwald eight months earlier. The raw memories of that time haunted him still. He had entered Buchenwald before the German guards had had chance to kill survivors in the camp. He saw for himself the piles of emaciated bodies in their grotesque positions, the half-dead skeletons of men, women and children barely moving around the camp.

As these terrible images were flashed before the world, again Howard prayed that his parents had been spared this suffering.

As the Nuremberg courtroom discussed the evidence, Howard was aware that Buchenwald was one of the largest concentration camps in Germany itself. A quarter of a million people had been taken there. Fifty-six thousand were killed by hard labour or starvation. It was located near Weimar, the cultural capital of Germany and home to the giant intellectuals: Goethe, Liszt and Nietzsche. The concentration camp was situated in the forest where Goethe wrote some of the finest German literature, including his famous work 'Faust'. Nazi brutality had not only desecrated German culture, but changed the land forever by the murder of millions of innocent lives. As Howard sat in the press section at the trial that day in December 1945, the irony of his position did not escape him. What was being shown in the court, he had seen first-hand. And now he was witnessing the process of justice. What went through his mind? He comments: 'Hanging the defendants was going to be much too quick a death for their crimes.'

Howard was familiar with what had gone on in concentration camps, what the Nazis had done to Jews during the 1930s and afterwards. He was an eyewitness to the systematic destruction of his people – of men, women and children who had considered themselves 'good Germans' for generations both before and during the war. Numerous personnel working at the Nuremberg Trial, some of whom were civilians, had come over from America. Howard felt that their experience of Nuremberg was different and coloured by the fact that they had not lived through the Nazi brutality. Not a criticism of them, but they had little understanding of how Nazism was carried through into the smallest facet of daily life. It is true that some of them had seen photographic evidence, but they had experienced it personally. Even with some knowledge of the Holocaust, for Howard's colleagues in the prison the evidence of sheer brutality and mass murder proved deeply shocking.

Howard is as clear today as he was in 1945 that the Nuremberg Trial was necessary to reveal to the world the inhumanity that had been committed in the name of Nazi supremacy. Nuremberg forced the German people to face the collective guilt of a nation.

'Nuremberg was a great consolation,' he says. 'It could not bring back any life that I had lost but it was satisfaction to have these monsters in a prison cell in front of me.'

Chapter Eight

CELL 1: HERMANN GOERING

I F ONE MAN was to stand out above all the defendants at Nuremberg it was Hermann Goering. For all his crimes, Goering remained a fascinating figure even in the jail cells. Hours of solitude behind prison walls could not diminish his spirit or sense of self-importance. He was a larger than life figure who appeared unphased by what lay ahead and the fact that he was on trial for his life. 'Germany had been totally defeated,' says Howard, 'and Goering knew he would face the gallows for his crimes, yet still he maintained his innocence. In freedom, Goering was a hunting man. Now the one-time hunter was the hunted.'

At the end of the war, as Soviet troops had marched closer to Berlin, Hermann Goering, one-time commander of the Luftwaffe and Hitler's deputy, had sent an urgent telegram to the Führer asking to be appointed leader of the Reich. Hitler's secretary Martin Bormann had intercepted the telegram and portrayed Goering's message to Hitler as treason. Hitler ordered Goering's, and execution along with his wife and daughter. Unknown to Hitler, the SS disobeyed orders and Goering fled to his childhood home Schloss Mauterndorf. On 9th May 1945, Goering gave himself up and surrendered to the American army in

Bavaria. Ever aware of his puffed-up importance, Goering surrendered in his Marshal's uniform with baton, side arms and dagger. He was searched and a lot of narcotics were found on him. Goering was taken first to Mondorf prison in Luxembourg, codenamed "Ashcan". From there, he was transferred to Nuremberg.

Graphic images of Buchenwald were fresh in Howard's mind as he walked down the specially constructed covered catwalk to the prison behind the main courthouse, and towards cell Number One. The prison, functional yet intimidating, finally gave him a sense of the enormity of what lay ahead. The wide corridor with cells on either side had one guard assigned to watch four cells. It was here on the ground floor that the main defendants were being kept for the duration of the trial. Circular staircases at both ends of the corridor led to two upper tiers where key Nazi witnesses were being held for interview. The walkways on the upper levels were fenced to avoid prisoners jumping to their deaths. A small square window in the center of each cell door was kept open at all times so the guards could watch for suicide attempts.

That September morning Howard kept his nerve as he followed Dr Kelley towards Hermann Goering's cell. The stark letters on the name plate on the door of cell Number One momentarily sent a shiver down Howard's spine as he and Kelley waited for the guard to turn the key. Howard would soon be face to face with the highest ranking surviving member of Hitler's former government. For all the abhorrence he felt for the crimes committed there was a strange sense of curiosity about the leaders themselves.

As the guard pushed open the heavy iron door, Howard had his first glimpse of the large imposing prisoner, sat on his bed. Howard's quick eye took in the confines of cell. Measuring 9ft by 13ft, it was simplistic with a bed fixed to the wall, which Americans called a cot. There was a toilet, small sink and a table with single chair. The defendants were allowed a few personal items: pencils, photographs and toiletries, but nothing which they could hang themselves. They were not allowed to wear their normal clothes but issued with special prison clothing. Hermann Goering who had arrived at Nuremberg with eighteen suitcases and a serious drug addiction was permitted one uniform stripped of rank and insignia, a change of clothing and some jewellery as long as he could not harm himself. Goering's several cases of jewellery and expensive gold watch was all that remained of the glitter of this once powerful man.

Colonel Andrus, who spent hours discussing the defendants' safety with his staff, ensured that even the table in the cell would collapse under the weight of the defendant if he sat on it. Whilst the defendants were out on exercise in the yard, the cells were regularly checked for anything hidden which they could use to harm themselves.

GOERING – THE FIRST ENCOUNTER

Goering's face seemed to light up when he saw Howard and Kelley enter as if he had been eagerly awaiting their visit. He patted the bed beside him for Kelley to sit down.

Kelley obliged, with notepad and pen poised ready to take down that morning's conversation. Goering's opening words were always the same: 'Good morning doctor. Good morning translator. I am glad you have come to see me.'

Howard pulled out the single wooden chair from the small table beside the bed, sat down and stared at Goering. The table displayed some very personal items: black & white photographs of the Goering family were propped against the wall. Three books lay flat on the desk, alongside a deck of cards and a few tiny boxes. It was an intimate snapshot of Goering's private life - the inner sanctum of 'Goering the man'. Howard reflected how, stripped of power, Goering seemed like any other family man.

Hermann Goering had been at the epicentre of Nazi policy in the 1930s. Howard could not possibly have known then that in less than a decade he would be talking to Goering in a jail cell. The turn-around was quite ironic. Hitler, Goebbels and Himmler were dead. Howard was alive and Goering was now behind bars. To be sitting within inches of the man who had wielded such power in the eyes of the German people in the 1930s seemed surreal. In Goering's cell that day, memories came flooding back of the times he had witnessed Goering at Nazi rallies in Munich with Adolf Hitler at the helm surrounded by his henchmen Joseph Goebbels and Heinrich Himmler. Through his thoughts, Howard heard Kelley's voice and came out of his reverie to start the translate work. This was the present and he had a job to do.

Kelley began to talk to Goering in a very relaxed manner. As Howard translated Goering's ramblings, it was immediately obvious that Goering adored the attention, even from his captors. The visit gave Goering time and space to express himself and his grandiose opinions of self-importance. Howard and Kelley heard it all. Goering had naïvely believed that by surrendering to the Allies, he would be received with open arms because he had not been closely associated with Hitler in the last months of the war. It was evident to Howard and Kelley that day that Goering had such a high opinion of himself that he believed the Allied Commanders would respect him and grant him the status of a defeated leader in exile, certainly not a war criminal. How wrong he was. His arrest landed him on the road to international accountability and justice.

Goering was already known to Kelley who had treated him for drug addiction in Mondorf prison. There Kelley had already begun to build a profile of his charge. As Hitler's deputy, Goering had carried out his public role with showy ease and enjoyment. Answerable only to Hitler, he had enjoyed unparalleled power not only as deputy, but Commander-in-Chief of the Luftwaffe (German air force), President of the Reichstag (parliament), Chairman of the Ministerial Council for the Defense of the Reich and Reich Governor of Prussia. Goering had completely controlled Germany's aviation. During the First World War, he had shown qualities of supreme leadership in the air force and been decorated with the *Pour le Mérite*, the highest German military award. A few years later in 1923, he was one of the leaders of the Munich Putsch when Hitler tried to overthrow the Bavarian government, ironically in the same city and year of Howard Triest's birth. During the failed coup, Goering was wounded in the thigh and spent almost a year in hospital. Twenty years later, sitting in the Nuremberg jail he could still display an irresistible charm when he chose to do so.

GOERING - THE PARADOX

Howard felt no pity for the man who had arrived at Nuremberg as a serious drug addict. An obese Goering, who weighed around 200 pounds in his early days in the prison, was a great orator but also a paradox. On the one hand, he was a huge collector of art who could be a brash, confident, self-centered man who loved his wife and could organize a great show at a party; on the other he was capable of sending millions to their deaths with no remorse.

Being a big showman tied in with Goering's whole life. He was always the bragger type in full uniform and regalia, a great hunter and opulent in everything he did. 'In the glimpses I had of him in parades in Nazi Germany in the 1930s,' says Howard, 'he was always decked in gold and jewels. Even in his prison cell when he wore a plain uniform devoid of all insignia, he was still the big show man; the man that had to be No.1. It was fortunate for him that Hitler was dead and now he could play No.1, which he did very well.'

This showman, unaccustomed as he was to defeat, had to face the total collapse of Nazi Germany and the world around him. It was not long before he started to explain the reasons for Hitler's defeat. He became very open with Howard and Kelley about the disagreements which had emerged between him and the Führer at the end of the war, telling them that only he of all the members in the Nazi hierarchy had dared to argue with the Führer. That led to a fundamental mistrust between him and Hitler. Howard and Kelley then heard firsthand Goering's own version of the events of the last days.

After Hitler had told his mistress, Eva Braun, and commander-in-chief, General Jodl, of his intended suicide, he had sent word to Goering that the end was near and that he, Hitler, intended to stay in the bunker in Berlin until the fight was over. Behind closed doors, Goering prepared to take over the reins of government and waited for notification of Hitler's death. But things went drastically wrong for Goering when a telegram which he sent to Jodl was shown to Hitler. Hitler believed that Goering was trying to seize power and ordered his arrest. On 23 April 1945, Goering answered a knock on the door to find his home surrounded by SS troops who immediately put him under house arrest.

On the evening of 29 April 1945, the day before Hitler's suicide, a telegram signed by Martin Bormann arrived with orders for the SS to kill Goering and his staff. Kaltenbrunner, one-time Gestapo Chief and another defendant being held a few cells away from Goering at Nuremberg, refused to carry out the death warrant without Hitler's signature on it. The execution was never carried out and Goering lived.

Now behind bars, Goering had hours a day in isolation to think about what had happened to Germany and where it had all gone wrong. What did he make of Hitler's suicide? He told Howard and Kelley that Hitler could not possibly have faced trial before a foreign court and preferred suicide to that. He admitted that Hitler had chosen the right course in taking his own life.

On the issue of war crimes, Goering was in complete denial. He was quite happy for the other defendants to be found guilty if it meant he walked free. Howard is blunt today when he recalls:

'We found Goering distancing himself from war crimes, denying any guilt, but in reality clearly at the heart of the extermination program. He felt he had done nothing wrong and that his actions were acceptable. He objected to the use of the term 'war crimes' and corrected Kelley by calling the atrocities "brilliant strategy". Neither did he recognize the legal jurisdiction of the Nuremberg courtroom and told Kelley so, but that would not stop Goering ultimately using the courtroom as an international stage to promote himself.'

Leaving Cell One that first day, Howard could not quite believe he had been so close to Goering. It would take a few more visits for reality to sink in.

In the coming days, Howard entered the cells of the other defendants for the first time. He and Kelley steadily built up a picture of the defendants and gradually became familiar with their idiosyncrasies. They did not visit every defendant every day, only those selected by Kelley. In the period immediately after the indictment was read by Airey Neave, they found Goering quite gloomy, but it didn't last long. Goering remained anything but defeated. He looked directly at Kelley during one visit, almost momentarily unaware of Howard's presence in the cell, and said, 'this is just like going into battle.' With this belligerent attitude, he faced the charges of war crimes. He reiterated to them that he was not a war criminal but a fiercely loyal German patriot.

'I did what I did for the sake of a greater Germany,' he told Kelley in German through Howard, 'I know I shall hang. You know I shall hang. I am ready.'

Kelley later wrote that Goering 'still possessed all the forcefulness, brutality, ruthlessness and lack of conscience which made him the ideal executive for Adolf Hitler.'

Goering became so trusting of Howard and Kelley that he confessed one day to having helped a Jewish family leave Nazi Germany. Goering told how he had maintained contact with a Jewish nurse who had helped him when he was wounded during the Munich Putsch of 1923. Because of her kindness, he personally aided her family with papers to leave Germany for England. Goering was keen to remind Howard and Kelley that if it wasn't for him, the nurse would have died in a concentration camp, but he was also quick to add that this was strictly a personal matter for him. Helping one Jewish family certainly did not change his overall view towards Jews.

Occasionally, Howard went into the cells on his own to interview the defendants. As the guard locked the door behind him, he faced them alone. There was no third person to take the pressure off the intimate setting. For Howard, it was initially an intimidating and isolating experience, but he hid his unease and nerves. He chose one such moment to ask Goering to sign a book that he had requisitioned from the library at Erlangen. That day, as usual, Goering was sitting on the edge of his bed, leaning forward deep in thought.

He looked up when Howard walked in and greeted him in his usual manner: 'Good day Mr Translator. So you have come to see me.' He noticed Howard was clutching a copy of his *Aufbau einer Nation*, a book which ran to over 200 pages.

Howard was not sure how Goering would react to signing it. In typical Goering style, he was flattered by the attention. From his point of view, Howard was an American soldier who was showing an interest in him as a person. It confirmed and reinforced his fundamental belief in his own self-importance and place in the history of Germany. As he was signing the book, he paused momentarily, looked up at Howard and proudly declared: 'I wrote this book over a weekend. That is quite an achievement, isn't it?'

He handed back the book. The inscription simply read: "Nuremberg 1946, Hermann Goering".

As Howard tucked the book under his arm, Goering nodded in acknowledgement and was particularly thoughtful. After an exchange of trivial pleasantries, Howard left the cell.

Walking back down the line of guards outside the cells, Howard reflected how Goering was the same man then as the start of his imprisonment: 'Never once did he portray to me or the psychiatrists the picture of a broken man. He was always the great Hermann Goering.'

CENSORING MAIL

During spare time between visits to the cells, Howard was given the job of censoring the defendants' mail. All their incoming and outgoing mail was written in German. Not speaking fluent German, Andrus needed to know what was being said in the correspondence and passed it to Howard.

What seemed an ordinary task could sometimes produce some unexpected humorous happenings. One day a particular packet arrived for Goering. There was the most awful smell of fish as Howard opened it to check its contents. Howard recalls:

'The "gift" sent to Goering that day was a dead herring. This for the man who had once boasted "if enemy planes ever fly over Berlin I will eat a dead herring". We never established who sent it, but it brought so much laughter to our office.'

Over the course of the trial, sack loads of mail arrived at the prison from members of the public, some of it from people deemed to be crazy by the prison authorities. Howard recalls that fan mail was never passed on. Colonel Andrus wanted in no way to given any of the defendants a sense that they were heroes or attracting publicity, however negative.

Goering again became an anomaly. His letters to his wife were exceptionally tender and loving and revealed the paradox that was Goering. 'He had the ability for great love,' says Howard, 'and yet he was the highest-ranking war criminal we had in the jail. He frequently complained to me that letters from his wife were all too infrequent.'

GOERING ON TRIAL

On the afternoon of 13 March 1946, Goering took the stand in the courtroom and represented himself. Taking centre stage, he milked the attention whilst in the stand. He made lengthy speeches to justify his position. By the third day, he had spoken for a total of twelve hours, all testimony from his perspective. The prosecutors fired questions at him about the planned extermination program of Jews. Howard recalls: 'In his defence, Goering argued that neither he nor Hitler knew anything about the plan to exterminate Jews. It leaves one wondering who he thought was responsible for the murder of six million Jews.'

The court heard in Goering's own words his attempt to explain the Nuremberg Laws of 1935 as 'a clear separation of the races' and 'to do away with the notion of persons of mixed blood.' The fact that the trial was taking place in the city where these laws were promulgated was not lost on those listening in the courtroom. Not once did Goering admit the slightest guilt for the crimes for which he was standing trial.

With the exception of Schirach, Funk, Speer and Doenitz, Goering even publicly denied knowing the other defendants before being with them at the trial. Distancing himself from the others would not fool the trial or make any difference to his sentence. For the duration of the trial, nothing changed Goering's belief that he would go down in the annals of German history as one of the country's greatest men. But now he was, as Goldensohn once commented, 'a Führer without a country, army or air force and on trial for war crimes.'

By May 1946 Goering, who was being visited frequently by Howard and Dr Goldensohn, became depressed. In his notes, Goldensohn recorded how Goering sat in his cell:

'smoking his long Bavarian hunting pipe and looking rather depressed when I entered with Mr Triest. He smiled forcibly in an attempt to appear cheerful and invited us to sit down.'

During this particular interview, Goering was still preoccupied with the defeat of Hitler which he continued to explain as a betrayal by those closest to the leader. He sat on the edge of his bed and bent over, staring at the floor. 'Then he suddenly sat upright,' says Howard. 'I could see he was concentrating hard on the questions I was translating from Goldensohn. Goering began to analyze the essential difference between himself and Hitler.'

'Let me explain,' Goering told Howard and Goldensohn, 'in one word the German people called him *my Führer*. They addressed me as Hermann. I was always closer to the hearts of the people than Hitler, but he was a great leader and I subscribed to his program completely. Naturally there are differences, which I am trying to get across to you and to the world, in that Hitler was a great man who was betrayed by some of his subordinates like Goebbels. Finally Hitler didn't know his real friends from his false ones. It was a great betrayal. The National Socialist program, in which I played no mean part, was a great reform movement which would have benefited Germany if the enemies of Hitler had not betrayed him.'

Goering was asked at what point he thought Germany had lost the war. Naturally, he had an opinion. In typical belligerent style, he declared that Germany's demise began with the Ardennes Campaign. He did not see the invasion of Sicily in the summer of 1943 or the Normandy landings in June 1944 as the beginning of the end.

In later interviews during May 1946, Goering's mood had changed and he welcomed company from Howard and Goldensohn. They broached the subject of Goering's childhood which he always maintained was irrelevant to his current fate. He was happy to discuss with them diverse subjects from the arts to philosophy and seemed pleased that the conversation had veered away from his guilt and war crimes. Howard recalls, 'Goering prided himself in being a man of culture. He undoubtedly saw himself as extremely refined in art, music and theatre.'

Goering had spent more than a decade plundering art from Europe. The walls of Carinhall, his country retreat not far from Berlin, displayed some of the finest paintings and masterpieces. Amongst those stolen by Goering were two works by Matisse: his *Still Life with Sleeping Women* and *Pianist and the Checker Players*, and Van Gogh's famous *Portrait of Dr Gachet*. As Allied forces pushed towards Germany at the end of the war, Goering moved stolen art by privately-hired trains to the Austrian border but the trains were intercepted. Some were hidden in salt mines in Austria and recovered in special missions by the Allies. The art was sent to Munich to be catalogued. Six decades later, much of it is thought to have been reclaimed by the original families and heirs or legitimately acquired by museums and galleries.

Towards the end of the trial, when Howard and Goldensohn went into Goering's cell, it was clear that he had accepted his fate. He knew then, as he did when Kelley was interviewing him nine months earlier, that he would be found guilty and hanged, but he was not revealing what was going through his mind.

Chapter Nine

CELL 9: ROBERT LEY

WITHIN TWO WEEKS of Howard arriving at Nuremberg, high drama broke out on the ground floor of the prison when defendant Robert Ley was found hanging in his cell. Ley, Hitler's chief of Labour Front, had managed to commit suicide even before the trial had opened. A bald, stocky short man, Ley had deputized for Hitler in the early days of Nazism when Hitler was unable to give particular speeches. Ley's last commission had been to organize the Hitler Free Corps to carry out guerrilla warfare against the advancing Allied forces.

In Nuremberg prison, Ley had given no cause for concern. Although he had made three minor suicide attempts immediately after capture by US forces, he had made no further attempts in his cell at Nuremberg. He was found to be intelligent with a good memory but unstable and fanatical. Instability was nothing unusual or unexpected amongst the accused. Kelley was able to carry out the Rorschach Ink Blot Test on Ley and concluded that he had physiological degeneration of the frontal lobes of the brain. That may have accounted for his behaviour in the cell. Neither Kelley nor Howard picked up the seriousness of Ley's increased agitation at the forthcoming trial. They were used to the accused 'letting off steam'. It was to be a sobering lesson.

Howard and Dr Kelley entered Cell 9 several times in the days immediately before the suicide. They found Ley unable to conduct a coherent conversation without gesticulating and ranting on. Ley noticeably lacked judgment which led Kelley to refer to him as an 'uninhibited rabble rouser'. Such a trait had enabled Ley to rally the masses to work for the greater good of the Third Reich and increase the labour forces several fold. Kelley suggested to Ley that he should write a short exposition to pass the time in the cell. The result was to be very revealing.

During one of Howard and Kelley's visits, Ley handed Kelley a copy of the finished piece which he called *Life or Fame? A Political Analysis*. The first half gives unqualified adoration for Hitler, in spite of the total defeat of the regime and all that had happened in the concentration camps. For Ley, Hitler's fame was 'unassailable.' He clung to a deluded adoration for Adolf Hitler and idolized his dead Führer almost as a god-like figure.

'The highest fame belongs to him,' wrote Ley, 'and he will appear to posterity as the shining hero of this period.' Of course, Ley was deluded and Hitler was not hailed a national hero.

Again, it was Major Airey Neave who entered Ley's cell to read the indictment, the crimes for which he was going to be tried. In it, he was accused of 'the abuse of human beings for labour in the conduct of aggressive wars.'

Neave advised Ley to seek a defence lawyer for the trial, as he had advised all the defendants. Ley barely looked at the indictment after it was handed to him. Other thoughts were running through his mind. Within a short time, he became extremely agitated and violently disturbed.

LEY BECOMES UNSTABLE

When Howard and Dr Kelley entered his cell on the day of the indictment, Ley was ranting and raving. What they did not foresee was that the prospect of the trial was becoming too much for him. Ley protested his innocence, as he did every time they entered his cell. He screamed that he had never killed anyone. Staring at Howard and Kelley with bloodshot eyes, he shouted that he was a patriotic German, not a war criminal. He shrieked in German, through Howard, that he would never stand trial. Neither Howard nor Kelley had seen Ley like this before. 'We thought he was just letting off steam and would eventually calm down,' says Howard, 'but the disturbance went far deeper.'

Dr Kelley recorded that day's events in his memoir, *22 Cells in Nuremberg*: 'In the middle of this tirade, he [Ley] marched dramatically to the far end of his cell, placed his back against the window, flung out his arms, and cried, "Shoot me! Now as a German! Don't try me as a common criminal".'

When Howard and Kelley visited again a few days later, Ley was asked how preparations for his defense were coming along.

Ley berated them: 'How can I prepare a defense? Am I supposed to defend myself against all these crimes which I knew nothing about? Hitler and I were only working for the good of the people. If, after all this bloodshed, some more sacrifices are needed to satisfy the vengeance of the victors, all well and good.'

Again, Howard witnessed Ley pleading with Kelley to shoot him. Neither realized the mental deterioration of this man so desperate to avoid the trial. Ley stood with his back against the cell wall, his arms outspread, begging to be shot. When Kelley again refused, Ley seemed to be calm for a moment as he quietly replied to Howard: "All well and good. You are the victors, but why should I be brought before a tribunal like a c...c...c...c..." At this point, he stammered so severely he was unable to continue. When Howard supplied the word "criminal", Ley added: "That's it. I cannot even get that word out."

Ley struggled more than most of the defendants over Germany's defeat. He held on to his unshakeable belief that Hitler would win the war so the disappointment for him was immense.

'As we sat with him in the cell, he had to face the fact that Germany's defeat was absolute,' explains Howard. 'Much of his disappointment soon turned into an angry rage against the Jews. Of course he did not know that I was Jewish.'

Howard and Kelley listened as Ley told them that he would have handled 'the Jewish problem' differently. He would not have killed them but forced them to emigrate by denying them homes and jobs. As leader of the Labour Front, he would have solved the problem for Hitler given the chance. With thoughts of suicide racing through his mind, Ley clutched at anything at the last minute to change the situation. In a moment of desperation and misplaced judgment, he tried to strike a bargain with Kelley. Through Howard as interpreter, he told Kelley that he hoped Kelley could unite with him to bring about a German-American

Alliance and the rebirth of Nazism. Ley was deluded because there was no possibility of that happening.

The day before Ley hanged himself, Howard entered the cell with both Dr Kelley and psychologist Dr Gilbert. The defendant was still in an extremely agitated state and launched into another tirade of anger. No one suspected *even now* that he was on the verge of taking his own life.

SUICIDE

The following day, 25 October 1945, Ley was found hanging from the toilet pipe in his cell. He had taken an army towel, made a noose by tying strips of the towel together and stuffed rags into his mouth to suppress any scream at the last moment of strangulation. It was a slow and painful death. Ley knew that, but was determined to avoid the trial at any cost.

It was clear that Colonel Andrus and other prison staff suffered total shock at the turn of events. Ley had succeeded in committing suicide even before the trial had opened. The only reference to Ley during the trial occurred during the first day of speeches in which it was acknowledged that Ley had 'succeeded in accomplishing his exit from the court of judgment and from the world of living men.'

Ley's unexpected suicide had ramifications for the whole prison regime. Colonel Andrus's first reaction was to allocate one guard to each cell, rather than a guard to every four cells. He was taking no chances on further suicides. Secondly, he did not circulate details of exactly how Ley died to avoid copy-cat cases. It did not prevent the defendants discussing his death at mealtimes. Goering was the most vocal and responded with some pleasure, saying he doubted Ley could have performed well at the trial. Only Streicher seemed disturbed and upset by it.

Every effort was made to ensure they did not replicate Ley's fate. All defendants were on 24-hour surveillance. The single light in their cell was kept on constantly, except it was dimmed at night to allow them to sleep. The cells were searched more thoroughly and they were not allowed belts, string or rope. The defendants were given regular body searches and had to sleep on their backs at night so the guards could see their head and hands at all times.

When the defendants left their cells to take meals together, daily exercise or attend the trial, they were under constant close observation. In the short period they spent together over meals, they could be heard planning their defence with Goering always assuming leadership.

Now that Ley was dead, Kelley was keen to undertake a post mortem of the brain to give a precise diagnosis and complete his study. Medical and psychological examinations while Ley was alive indicated some kind of organic brain damage, but Kelley was eager to verify further. Colonel Andrus granted Kelley's request. Kelley summarized his findings as: 'brain damage of the deteriorating type in the front lobe area, verifying the diagnosis and accounting for Ley's peculiar behaviour as Labour Leader of the Reich.'

With the brain removed, Ley's body was taken from the prison for burial by German undertakers. It was transported to an undisclosed cemetery in an open box lined with butcher's paper. In the cemetery and exposed to the elements, the open box rested next to a newly dug grave until two elderly gravediggers turned up to bury him. With no remnant of respect left for Ley, even in death, the gravediggers unceremoniously tipped his body out of the box into the deep grave. Ley's body fell with a thump into the wet earth face down, a piece of the butcher's paper stuck to his back. The precise location of his body has never been disclosed. Today few people, except historians of Nuremberg, have heard of Robert Ley or know who he was.

Back at the prison, day to day life there in the autumn of 1945 lacked the drama of the first two weeks of October 1945. Colonel Andrus continued to blame himself for Ley's death for failing to station a sufficient watch guard over the defendants. In spite of implementing strict procedures and measures, it would not later prevent a determined Hermann Goering from taking a cyanide pill just hours before his scheduled execution the following autumn.

CHAPTER TEN

CELL 25: JULIUS STREICHER

A S HITLER'S DIRECTOR of Propaganda, Julius Streicher was arguably the most anti-Semitic of all the defendants. At Nuremberg, he made a lasting impression on Howard Triest. Streicher hated Jews with an unnatural viciousness and vengeance. The contents of his vehemently anti-Semitic propaganda newspaper *Der Stürmer* portrayed stereotypical cartoons of how to recognize a Jew by their facial features. These cartoons were reinforced with anti-Semitic rhetoric. As a young boy Howard had seen the newspaper displayed in noticeboards behind glass on street corners everywhere in Munich. It served as a visual reminder, as if he needed it, of how bad things were becoming for Germany's Jews.

In Cell 25, Streicher was as obsessed by anti-Semitism as in the early years of the regime. Total defeat of Nazism had done nothing to change that. When Howard entered the cell with Dr Kelley for the first time, Streicher was sat on his bed reading the Bible. The balding, stocky man from Bavaria was not reading this holy text out of any religious motives but because he wanted to show how the Jews' own scriptures had already condemned them. Howard and Kelley soon discovered that he knew the Bible thoroughly.

Streicher put the book down and waited for Kelley to speak. Kelley began his questioning and Howard translated. Streicher soon veered off the questions and onto his lengthy explanations of 'the Jewish problem'. It was soon apparent that he was entirely consumed by it. Little realizing that Howard was Jewish, Streicher explained how the true danger still lay with the Jews.

Dr Kelley quickly picked up that Streicher was displaying a different reaction to their questioning than the other defendants. Streicher was found to be exclusively driven by emotion, which was why Howard and Kelley concentrated on his case and visited him so frequently. There was something different about the defendant in cell 25 that was not just down to instability. Howard and Kelley listened patiently as Streicher explained how in the early days of the Nazi Party he had realized the true danger of Jews and joined along with others to fight the Jews. Howard recalls:

> 'We found Streicher polite, but irrational, often fiery-tempered but sometimes uncouth and abrasive in his tone. Everything he believed about Jews was based on emotion, not fact. He raved on to us about the destructive power of Jews in society, in government and on the international stage. From what I witnessed of him, and we got to know him very well, he was more anti-Semitic and fanatical than Adolf Hitler.'

Streicher argued irrationally that Germany's defeat was not down to Hitler but international Jewry. He also believed that the Nuremberg Trial was brought about by propaganda from the Jewish Press. The eyes of the world were on the trial with massive media coverage, and that for him was the result of Jewish influence. Streicher said he knew this. The trial was, for him, a platform in which he could convince the world that international Jewry was the real threat.

In another interview, he enlarged on the theme that he was being sacrificed. 'The entire history of the world has proven,' he ranted, 'that the bearers of truth and understanding are always a minority. I am one of that small group. The knowledge of belonging among the pioneers of the truth gives me the inner strength to survive all hardships of these trying times.'

THE 'ARYAN' FRIEND

Perhaps the most extraordinary part of Howard's story is the personal relationship that developed over twelve months between him and Streicher. The sixty-one year old war criminal with pinched moustache, who had demanded representation only from a non-Jewish lawyer, boasted to Howard:

'I can smell a Jew a mile away. I can see it in their face, their eyes, their hair, from the way they walk, even the way they sit. And I know you are a pure Aryan and your people must have come from a Nordic country.'

This turned out to be the biggest irony of all. Streicher himself did not have the pure Aryan look as defined by his own newspaper. Neither did it occur to him to question Howard's Jewishness because Howard had blond hair and blue eyes. Howard's "Aryan" looks were something which had saved him many times during the 1930s and had enabled him to walk unnoticed through the streets of Munich without being arrested.

Now, of all the staff working at Nuremberg, the defendant in Cell 25 embraced Howard as his 'Aryan friend'. In his blind prejudice, Streicher assumed the psychiatrists to be Jewish because they were serving in a 'Jewish profession', but not Howard. Of the psychiatric team in the prison, Kelley was not Jewish. The question 'Are you Jewish?' was never asked by Streicher of Howard. Streicher was fooled for a year.

In an unexpected twist, Streicher turned to Howard as his new 'Aryan friend' and began to entrust things to him. Howard and Kelley entered the cell one day to find Streicher fretting over personal papers which he did not want to fall 'into Jewish hands'. Streicher looked at Kelley directly and said that he had some notes on the 'Jewish question' which needed translating but he felt a Jew would falsify the translation. He instructed Kelley to find a good Aryan to translate it.

'Then he paused,' says Howard, 'suddenly turned to me and passed me the papers and said, "Here – you do the translating. You're a good German."'

With some wry amusement, Howard left the cell that day, clutching Streicher's treasured papers and handed them straight to Colonel Andrus. Howard did not feel it his place to read them, but the incident revealed the deep mistrust which Streicher had for Kelley whom he wrongly assumed him to be Jewish. Kelley wrote about the incident in his autobiography:

'Streicher himself fanatically believed that one could tell a Jew by his physical characteristics. He couldn't, of course. One of my top interpreters was a German refugee [Howard] who had escaped from Germany in 1939. Like many other German Jews, he was typically "Nordic" in appearance – blond hair, blue eyes, slender athletic body.'

Colonel Andrus, too, found the relationship between Streicher and Howard important enough to mention in his autobiography when he wrote:

'He [Streicher] was obsessed with anti-Semitism, even though he had gone through a temporary reformation. The tribunal had an interpreter, a pleasing little man – a Jew – who had, oddly, yellow hair and blue eyes. He was authorized to go to the cell-block to add to the knowledge the Allies were collecting on religious persecution. It was not for presentation in court but merely for the record. Streicher was delighted to see this man with the fair hair and expressed delight in him as a "perfect example of a German Nordic". He trembled with rage as he mentioned Jews, while quietly this Jewish officer sat before him taking notes.'

THE PAPER DOLL

One particular female Lieutenant working in the prison continually taunted Streicher about his impending fate.

She never entered his cell, but peered through the small open window in the cell door. Taking from her pocket a paper-cut-out doll with string around its neck, she dangled it in front of Streicher. 'Each time she did so, it sent Streicher into an absolute rage,' recalls Howard.

Watching her do this one day, Howard believed it served no purpose to treat any of the defendants with contempt, in spite of what they had done to millions of innocent victims. It was not right to lower themselves to the same level as the Nazis. Howard knew how Streicher would react and that the Lieutenant's action was inappropriate for a prison keeper.

Streicher was not going to be beaten by her. The next time she dangled the paper doll, he turned around, pulled down his trousers and showed his rear end at her. When Howard visited Streicher that same day, he was still enraged by the incident and referred to the Lieutenant with disdain as 'that Jew girl'. It is not known whether she was Jewish, but nevertheless Streicher claimed she was because, as he told Howard, 'she has a large Jewish nose.'

PRESERVATION OF JEWISH BOOKS

The questions directed by Kelley at Streicher were diverse, designed to understand Streicher the man. He was asked about his famous collection of pornography which he boasted was the largest collection in the world and, apparently, all confiscated from Jews. His obsession with pornography disgusted the other defendants who petitioned the guards to allow them to eat their meals separately from him. Their request was denied. The anomaly was not lost on Howard. The other defendants, about to stand trial for unimaginable evil and genocide, were trying to display a hierarchy of morals in the prison. Even more bizarre was the revelation that Streicher had the largest collection of rare Jewish books in Germany.

Whenever a synagogue had been desecrated or a rabbi's home searched, Streicher had ordered the removal of the books to the library building of his newspaper *Der Stürmer*. From these confiscated books, he selected the rarest and best. Instead of burning them alongside other books of a 'degenerate' nature, they survived. The shelves of Streicher's library which weighed heavy with Jewish literature were ironically kept in a building in Nuremberg that survived Allied bombing. How ironic, then, that the biggest Jew-baiter in Germany had, in effect, preserved for posterity a large share of the most famous and rarest literature of the German Jews.

Trying to understand what made Streicher tick was never going to be easy. He applied the same obsessive behaviour towards anti-Semitism, Jewish literature and pornography as his own personal hygiene. In the jail, he was neurotically impeccable in his appearance. He kept himself meticulously clean in spite of the primitive prison conditions. Word filtered back from the guards to Howard and Kelley that Streicher rose in his cell around 6am every morning to wash in a bucket of cold water. This he did even in the midst of winter. It was noted that none of the other defendants paid such rigorous attention to their own personal cleanliness. Streicher's behaviour caused Kelley to conclude that medically: 'he, along with defendant Rudolf

Hess, was unstable and suffered from the same sporadic paranoiac behaviour.'

STREICHER'S FATE

With the trial well underway, Streicher was under no illusion about his fate. He told Howard: 'I expect to be found guilty, but I am glad that the court at least pretends to be fair, because I may have a chance to testify and reveal to the world the true structure of the International Jew and to warn the world of this outstanding menace.' He explained to Howard and Kelley that his aim had been to rebuild Germany and it was he who was the vanguard of truth.

Of Streicher, the British Prosecution said: 'for twenty-five years he educated the German people in the philosophy of hate, of brutality, or murder. He incited and prepared them to support the Nazi policy, to accept and participate in the brutal persecution and slaughter of his fellow men.'

Streicher was the first of the defendants to inscribe a book to Howard. On 13 December 1945, Howard had gone into his cell alone, confident that Streicher would not object to his request – by now having gained his total trust. Armed with a copy of *Hofjuden*, he entered the cell. Streicher noticed the book immediately. Eying Howard as an ally, he gave a rare smile.

'Would you sign it?' Howard asked. Streicher didn't even hesitate and reached for the book. Without a word, Howard passed it to him and watched as Streicher bent over scrawling inside the words: 'Mr Howard Triest, in memory! Nuremberg 13.12.45, Julius Streicher.'

The second book, *Kampf dem Weltfeind*, Streicher signed with the same inscription two months later, dated 3 February 1946. On both occasions, as Streicher handed back the books, he took the opportunity to ramble on about what was on his mind. Howard comments:

> 'We talked together in a relaxed way. The only reason he talked freely to me was because he didn't know I was Jewish. He had my full attention and launched into one of his anti-Semitic speeches. I just sat and listened. I had heard it all before. Every now and again he would look up at me to see if I was still paying attention. Streicher was one of the few who really didn't change his anti-Semitic statements.'

As the trial progressed, Streicher maintained his innocence and saw only the other defendants as culpable of war crimes. He was found guilty by the court and sentenced to death by hanging. On 16 October 1946, Streicher died on the gallows never knowing that his 'Aryan friend' at Nuremberg was a Jew he would readily have sent to the death camps.

CHAPTER ELEVEN

RUDOLF HESS: THE BORDERLANDS OF INSANITY

HOWARD HAD ONLY been in the prison a few days when Rudolf Hess, Adolf Hitler's deputy prior to 1941, was brought to Nuremberg from England. It was 10 October 1945. The day is still vivid in his mind:

> 'Hess caused such a commotion that we all knew he had arrived. Flanked by guards, he was still in Luftwaffe uniform stripped of insignia and wearing long black flying boots. In the corridor he passed Goering, also surrounded by guards. Hess gave the Hitler salute. Colonel Andrus reacted immediately and said to him: 'Never do that in my prison again!'

Although Hess was in an agitated state and hyper alert, he was physically in good shape. Kelley was keen to examine him straight away, so he and Howard entered Hess's cell.

Of all the defendants, Hess proved the most difficult and unbalanced. He spoke English quite well and was questioned by Kelley mainly in English. At other times, questions were directed to him in German, depending on the type of question and whether it required a detailed answer which would be best given in his native language. Hess cooperated during questioning, but frequently responded that he could not remember the answer. This applied, for example, to his date and place of birth, and the date he had left Germany for England. His minders in England, the British Secret Service (SIS), had found the same, i.e. that he was prone to periods of amnesia, paranoia and neuroticism.

Hess had flown alone to England in a Messerschmitt 110 on 10 May 1941 to negotiate peace. He had bailed out over Scotland and, on landing, was immediately arrested by the authorities. He was held in a number of secure places during his internment in Britain, including four days in the Queen's House at the Tower of London. While in British custody, he became convinced that the authorities were trying to poison him and was frequently visited by army doctors and psychiatrists to assess his condition.

Hess was the highest ranking Nazi to be captured by the British during the war. It was considered quite a coup, except as time went by, it soon became clear that he could offer nothing substantial by way of intelligence about the Nazi war machine. Hess had been a key figure from the early days of the Nazi Party and, at that point, second only to Hitler in the Third Reich. He had been involved in Hitler's failed Putsch in Munich in 1923, was arrested then and charged with seizing several Bavarian hostages. He served a prison sentence with Hitler in Landsberg jail where Hitler wrote his infamous anti-Semitic book, *Mein Kampf*. It was during their incarceration there that Hess acted as Hitler's secretary and took down most of *Mein Kampf* while also influencing Hitler's belief in a possible German conquest of Europe and even the world.

FEIGNED MADNESS?

'By the time Hess came to us at Nuremberg,' says Howard, 'he was introverted and a bit of a nutcase. It was hard to penetrate him or build up any kind of rapport. He never said very much in his cell. He was a strong but quiet, nondescript person who looked at you with staring eyes. He turned out to be the quietest of all the defendants. When he did speak, it was to tell us why he had decided to fly solo to England under the false name Alfred Horn.'

Once in Nuremberg, it was Kelley's job to assess whether the paranoia was genuine or feigned. Initially, it was thought Hess was faking madness to avoid the death sentence, but Kelley concluded that sometimes the paranoia was phoney, sometimes real. During the absences of amnesia, Hess displayed anger when asked about his internment in England and quickly became agitated by the frequent military questions which Kelley asked him.

'Through all this,' says Howard. 'Hess remained a fervent supporter of Hitler. Nothing changed that. And he clung to a fundamental mistrust of both myself and Kelley.'

'You are kind, yes,' Hess told them, 'But I do not know if you are a friend.' When He was examined the day after his arrival at Nuremberg, again he appeared not to remember his capture, internment in England or arrival in the prison. He refused to take any medication or allow Kelley to undertake any hypnosis. Howard recalls:

'Hess became depressed and morbid. It was a priority to keep him fit for trial so we spent many hours with him in those early days. Kelley had a difficult job with Hess, and not wanting to rely solely on his own judgment and findings, he requested further professional opinions. Colonel Andrus authorized Hess to be examined by ten visiting psychiatrists: three Russian, three British, one French and three American.'

The psychiatrists were unanimous in agreeing with Kelley's diagnosis of amnesia. The focus shifted to keeping Hess as level as possible so he could take the stand in the courtroom. The American prosecutor, Justice Robert Jackson, advised Kelley against prescribing any drugs to Hess because if anything happened to Hess, it could be blamed on the treatment.

CLAIMS OF POISONING

While in the prison, Hess carried on the deluded belief that the authorities were trying to poison him via his food. On occasion, Howard went into the cell alone. He found Hess totally preoccupied with the issue of poisoning: 'He was suspicious of everything and everyone around him, although generally he did not react too much to me. The guards let me into his cell and I found a vacant-looking Hess standing by his desk.'

On the desk were a handful of miniature parcels containing samples of cocoa, coffee, tea or part of a meal. Hess carefully wrapped the samples in envelopes and neatly labelled each one. He passed some of them to Howard and instructed him to have them analysed. On leaving the cell, Howard immediately went to Andrus's officer and handed most of them over. Some parcels, Howard kept and took back to the United States in 1947, but over the years they have been lost.

'The irony of the whole poisoning phobia', says Howard, 'was that Hess outlived all the defendants.'

At the earliest opportunity, Kelley carried out a series of psychological tests on Hess to assess his IQ. This included the Rorschach Ink Blot Test. On the day of the test, Howard followed Kelley into the cell. Hess was sitting on his bed. On this occasion, Kelley sat down on one side of him, Howard on the other. Kelley took out the cards and began to show them in a particular sequence. As Hess responded, Howard translated and Kelley took down copious notes. Howard recalls:

'Hess seemed surprisingly relaxed as we carried out the test, eager to do his best. The test enabled Kelley to pay close attention to his reactions and behaviour. I remember that the cards showed Hess's tendency towards introversion, morbidity and obsession.'

For all Hess's instability, the result of the Rorschach Ink Blot Test was surprising. Kelley concluded that he was above average intelligence, with an IQ result between 115 and 120. Taking these results with the other intelligence tests carried out and his own observations, Kelley summarized his findings on Hess as suffering from: 'a true psychoneurosis, primarily of the hysterical type, engrafted on a basic paranoid and schizoid personality, with an amnesia.'

While Hess was not deemed insane during the months Kelley examined him, he was certainly a possible candidate for an asylum. His displays of paranoia were frequently accompanied by childish and hysterical behaviour, causing Kelley to conclude that Hess lived in 'the borderlands of insanity'.

FIT TO STAND TRIAL

As the trial progressed, the psychiatric team based in the prison was keen to assess the defendants' reactions to the day's evidence and legal proceedings. After returning to their cells, some defendants were immediately visited by Howard and the psychiatrist. Hess was one of the defendants that they kept under continuous, close surveillance. His behaviour called into question his fitness to stand trial and constituted a headache for the prosecuting Counsel.

In spite of episodes of delusion, amnesia and paranoia, Hess was deemed fit enough to stand trial. In the end, he entered the dock along with the other defendants. However, his behaviour in the prison ultimately affected his verdict.

On 30 November 1945, he entered the witness box and made his famous statement which confirmed Dr Kelley's findings. Hess told the court, 'my memory is in order again. The reason why I simulated loss of memory was tactical.'

As soon as word reached Kelley that Hess was back in his cell after that day's proceedings, he and Howard headed straight to see him. Instead of finding him in his usual subdued state after a long day in court, he was 'a bit like a zombie.' Howard recalls: 'but on this day, he was very different. He was extremely alert and proud of his statement in court.'

Hess stared at Howard and Kelley and said: 'How did I do? Good, wasn't I? I really surprised everybody, don't you think?'

Kelley shook his head and said, 'not everybody.' Hess had not fooled Kelley. It was as if he was playing a game with Kelley and knew exactly what he was doing. Hess's condition ultimately caused Kelley to conclude, 'if one considers the street as sanity and the sidewalk as insanity, then Hess spent the greater part of his time on the curb.'

Hess's condition did not improve during Goldensohn's period as psychiatrist in the prison. On one occasion, Goldensohn and Howard entered his cell to find him sat at his desk, scribbling in German. Goldensohn indicated to Howard to take a look. Hess didn't seem to mind as Howard picked up the paper and read the page. It was Hess's own rules for keeping himself healthy. With his known obsessions and paranoia, the notes reveal a preoccupation, even insecurity, with getting it right. They read in translation:

'Eat little. Don't take any sleeping pills. They will only lose the effect in case that you should really need them. Also take little other medicine [analgesics]. Instead of egg, ask for marmalade and bread. Don't eat or drink in the morning in order not to get tired. Ask the doctor for orange or lemon juice every once in a while. Don't eat salty food. Otherwise the cramps may become more frequent.'

In the end, Hess proved to be a total paradox – the Rorschach Test had shown that. The Hess affair made the job of the psychiatrists doubly difficult in trying assess or understand him. Uppermost in the mind of the Allied prosecutors was avoiding a diagnosis that would prevent Hess from seeing the trial through to its conclusion. In the end, the state of Hess's mental health affected the verdict in court because he was sentenced to life imprisonment rather than death by hanging.

CHAPTER TWELVE

THE POLITICAL MEN

T HE POLITICAL MEN in Adolf Hitler's regime found themselves unexpectedly indicted on charges of war crimes. In the weeks leading up to Germany's crushing defeat in 1945, they did not expect to be high on the list of wanted war criminals. In their own eyes, they were nothing more than administrators who carried out orders from above, and as such, could not possibly be implicated in mass murder. They were proved wrong. The Allies saw it differently, hunted them down and brought them to Nuremberg. They were: Joachim von Ribbentrop, Wilhelm Frick, Walther Funk, Hans Fritzsche, Alfred Rosenberg, Ernst Kaltenbrunner, Franz von Papen, Fritz Sauckel, Albert Speer, Baldur von Schirach, Fritz Sauckel, Konstantin von Neurath, Hjalmar Schacht and Artur Seyss-Inquart. These men left less of an impression on Howard than Goering, Streicher and Höss. Nevertheless, the military men were on the list of regular visits from the prison psychiatrist and his interpreter, Howard.

VON RIBBENTROP

When Howard and Kelley first visited Joachim von Ribbentrop in his cell, they found him depressed, uncontrolled and in a helpless state. Kelley attributed this to emotional instability caused by the lack of communication with his wife and family, as well as the loss of his Fuhrer. Life was not supposed to be easy for these war criminals. Many missed their families, and prison visits from the wives were severely restricted. Yet in spite of outward display of restlessness and torment, von Ribbentrop displayed no remorse. As Germany's foreign minister, he had moved in the highest social circles abroad. His affair with American divorcée Wallis Simpson, mistress of Edward VIII and future bride for whom Edward relinquished his throne, caused controversy and concern in British royal circles. Von Ribbentrop knew how to charm, particularly the ladies, and could hold court as the smart diplomat. His cell in Nuremberg was a world away from the glamour of socialite London that he had so enjoyed in the 1930s. the contrast could not have been starker.

During his imprisonment, von Ribbentrop's appearance became slovenly and messy. Howard recalls, 'his cell was the most untidy in the entire jail. He was totally disorganized, indecisive and in a muddle. When we visited him, he would be pacing the room, up and down, through a pile of crumpled papers strewn across the floor, and wringing his hands.'

The conversation frequently turned to Hitler and at this point von Ribbentrop became extremely fanatical. Howard said nothing as he sat on the bed beside him, while von Ribbentrop let off steam. Kelley, and later Goldensohn, furiously scribbled in the notebook. Like the other defendants, von Ribbentrop had invested all his belief and energy in the Führer whose regime had been disclosed to the world at Nuremberg in all its graphic and horrific detail. He, like the other defendants, found it difficult to face reality. During these times, he ardently repeated the words: 'I have always stood behind the Führer and always will.' This was quickly followed by a qualified remark that, although he followed Hitler on everything, he had nothing to do with his mass extermination program and as such was not guilty of any crimes. Howard recalls:

'He took the same line as the other defendants in denying any guilt for the atrocities committed by the Nazi regime. He told us that he had taken no part in the mass exterminations and murder in the concentration camps – these, he explained to us, were to do with Nazi domestic policy and not foreign policy. As Foreign Minister, he thought he could disavow any involvement in domestic affairs. That view would ultimately not convince the court that he was innocent. Von Ribbentrop remained fiercely loyal to Hitler to the end.'

In the last few visits which Howard made to von Ribbentrop's cell, the defendant began to look a very sick man. 'There was a tremendous change in him,' says Howard. 'He became pale and yellow skinned. Sometimes he looked quite ashen and unwell. He certainly did not behave like the former boisterous Foreign Minister.'

THE KILLING MACHINE

Sixty-nine year old defendant Wilhelm Frick, Minister of Interior for ten years from 1933 until 1943, faired no better than von Ribbentrop. Speaking in clipped German to the psychiatrist through Howard, he too disavowed himself of any guilt in the atrocities committed by the regime. In interviews, Goldensohn focused on Frick's family background in an attempt to understand him.

In another cell was Walther Funk, former Minister of Economics. As such, he had been responsible for drawing up laws which allowed for the confiscation of Jewish businesses. Howard comments:

> 'Funk told us that confiscating Jewish businesses was a very different matter from exterminating Jews. His claim to innocence was much harder to defend when it was known that one of the key Nazi witnesses at Nuremberg, Otto Ohlendorf, had worked for him for a year.'

On Ohlendorf's own admission, he had worked in death squads and killed around 90,000 Jews. Funk always maintained to Howard and Kelley that he knew nothing of Ohlendorf's killings nor of Nazi atrocities. This conviction motivated him to spend several hours a day in his cell at a type-writer, preparing his defence and disassociating himself from Ohlendorf and acts of atrocities by other Nazi leaders. When Howard and Goldensohn interviewed Funk in April 1946, he was still engrossed in typing up his defence. He tried to give them a coherent explanation of the elimination of Jews from economic life in Germany. And yet, as if to distance himself from war crimes, he claimed that he had nothing to do with the extermination of Jews. He even argued that some of his closest friends were Jews. As with the other prisoners, Funk knew nothing of Howard's own Jewish background.

Funk was asked: 'why did you stay on as Minister of Economics until the end of the war?' His patriotic reply: 'for the sake of Germany.' For Funk it was that simple. He said: 'I am guilty of one thing – that I should have cleared out and not had anything to do with these criminals in the first place.' Today Howard reflects on Funk's comment and says: 'This was easy to say in hindsight in a jail cell with his life on the line.'

During January 1946, forty-six year old Hans Fritzsche was interviewed several times by Howard and Goldensohn. The interviews centred on questions about Fritzsche's family background, in an attempt to construct of a biographical profile of him. Like Funk, Fritzsche was also busy typing up his defence for the courtroom. When Howard and Goldensohn entered his cell, he was quite content to stop typing and talk. Like the other defendants, he searched the past to find something redeeming, as if it would erase the charges against him or lessen his sentence. For Fritzsche, the redemptive story in his life was when he helped a Jewish man from Pomerania. He recounted how one day a woman in distress had come into his office because her husband had been imprisoned by the Gestapo. Fritzsche explained how he battled for three or four months to secure his release from a concentration camp, and that the man was only part Jewish, having had a Jewish grandfather – as if that made it easier.

Fritzsche believed he had been duped by both Hitler and Goebbels. Like the others, he claimed he knew nothing of the war crimes and the mass murder of Jews. In typical fashion, he blamed those who were no longer alive. 'Interestingly, Fritzsche had his own view of Hermann

Goering,' recalls Howard, 'He told us that Goering was not responsible for the mass murders like the other leaders, but that he certainly knew about the crimes.'

Fritzsche found it hard to accept his incarceration. Neither could he settle into prison routine. Having had no news from his wife and child, he became depressed. Consequently, when Howard and Goldensohn visited him on 6 April 1946, he was pleased to have a reprieve from solitary confinement and his own morbid thoughts. They found him frustrated. but philosophical. He told them: 'I have the feeling during this year of internment and half a year of trial that I have endured, a spiritual suffering and depression more terrible than death.' The problem for Fritzsche was his failure to really understand why he was standing trial. He told Howard: 'Sometimes I feel like screaming here in my cell. It isn't just my life that's ruined and frustrated. It's the guilt to my family and to the German people as a whole.'

During interviews the following month, he was still found to be frustrated by his imprisonment. By May, he continued to deny any knowledge of atrocities committed by the Third Reich, but did admit to an exception - he said he knew about Hitler's order that captured Allied pilots should be killed. This was followed by an explanation of how the Jews were responsible for the war, but having made that admission, he was at pains to say that he was no anti-Semite like Streicher.

Fritzsche did not think too highly of Streicher and abhorred his use of pornography in the *Der Stürmer* newspaper. He recounted how he and Goebbels had tried to ban the paper. A few days later, Fritzsche told them:

'As far as the indictment is concerned, accusing me of murder and inhumanity, I do not feel guilty. I don't feel guilty because I was betrayed. The only guilt I feel is in having trusted and believed Hitler and Goebbels and other people who did not warrant such trust.'

ROSENBERG, VON PAPEN AND KALTENBRUNNER

To a young Howard, fifty-year old defendant Alfred Rosenberg, one time racial philosopher of the Nazi party, looked anything but a mass murderer. And yet, as Reichsminister of the Eastern Occupied Territories, Rosenberg epitomized Nazi brutality and the extermination program. Kelley later wrote of him:

'As an administrator, Rosenberg failed miserably; as an exterminator, he succeeded almost beyond belief. In captured documents, I found evidence that he had literally millions of the inhabitants of the area either deported or exterminated. There is little doubt that conquered Russian territories suffered more under Rosenberg than any other area under Nazi domination.'

The observation by Howard himself that the accused looked like anyone's kindly grandfather, and not men of evil, remained a challenge during his time in Nuremberg Prison.

Ernst Kaltenbrunner, one-time head of the Reich Security office, had been responsible for the torture of enemies of the Nazi regime. An evil man, he claimed that he was not a war criminal because he had not personally killed anyone. That would not count for anything when he stood in the witness box in the courtroom. In his diary notes for 6 June 1946, Goldensohn wrote:

'Kaltenbrunner was in his usual inhibited, frigid state. He was superficially polite and expressed pleasure at the visit of Mr Triest and myself. He remarked that I had not been in to see him for a few weeks and, "I wondered whether you had become disgusted with us war criminals – particularly me, the so-called arch criminal of them all".'

Franz von Papen, Hitler's Vice Chancellor and a slick diplomat, was first visited only by Dr Kelley and Dr Gilbert. The reason for this is unclear. Dr Kelley wrote of von Papen: 'his attitude is perfectly rational, and his basic personality must be considered as entirely normal, except for his inability to abide by the accepted code of honesty and loyalty, either in word or act.'

Only months later, and accompanying Goldensohn, did Howard go into von Papen's cell. He now has no vivid memories of these interviews, perhaps because von Papen did not cut much of a character. This was true also for interviews carried out with the other defendants Baldur von Schirach (former Gauleiter of Vienna),

Albert Speer (Minister of Defence), Arthur Seyss-Inquart (Reichskommissor of the Netherlands and deputy to Hans Frank in Poland), Konstantin von Neurath (Hitler's Foreign Minister in Czechoslovakia) and Fritz Sauckel (second-in-command to Albert Speer and Gauleiter of Thuringia. Sauckel was complicit in war crimes having supplied an estimated 10 million slave workers from 1942–1945 to industrial firms like Krupp. None of these defendants had the forceful, memorable character that Goering or Streicher exhibited in the cells.

CHAPTER THIRTEEN

THE BEASTS OF POLAND

TWO MEN NICKNAMED the 'beasts of Poland' were brought into Nuremberg Prison approximately six months apart. They were Hans Frank and Rudolf Höss, both aged forty-six. Hans Frank was the first to be arrested in the summer of 1945 and was one of the twenty-two defendants being held in the prison. The second, Rudolf Höss, was the former Commandant of Auschwitz who was finally arrested by British forces in March 1946 and brought originally to Nuremberg as a witness in the trial. Contact with these two men was arguably amongst the most difficult and disturbing moments for Howard. Sitting next to them in their cells, not once did Howard let down his guard. He was to hear terrifying details of the inner daily workings of the Nazi killing machine.

Within the confines of a tiny cell Howard faced the men who were ultimately responsible for his parents' deaths. Höss was already the commandant of Auschwitz when Howard's parents arrived there on the train from Camp Drancy in 1942. He was probably there to 'greeted' the train. How chilling this knowledge was for Howard as he listened to Höss's detailed explanations of the killings and yet displayed no remorse.

HANS FRANK

Hans Frank was different from the other defendants in that he was the only one who showed some remorse during his time in prison. During the trial, he became very religious and, on 25 October 1945, underwent a Roman Catholic baptism in his cell. Howard observed that, in a strange way, Frank was removed from reality, aloof and withdrawn from everything around him. As a result of this change in his character, he reacted badly to the films of atrocities being shown in the courtroom. One day, Frank came close to being the only defendant to ask Howard about his background: 'He asked me and Kelley one day if we were Catholic. We both said, no – which was true. So he never discovered my Jewish background.'

How ironic too that Frank signed a copy of *Rechtsgrundlegung des Nationalsozialistischen Fuehrer Staates* to Howard and simply wrote inside the book: 'In memoriam, Frank.'

As Gauleiter of Poland, Frank was responsible for the deportation and deaths of millions of Jews. He had been captured on 3 May 1945 and immediately made a suicide attempt by slashing his throat, wrist and arm. The cut on his throat was quite superficial however damage to the left wrist and hand caused some paralysis. He made no further suicide attempts while in the jail. Although he showed penitence in his cell he denied any knowledge of the atrocities in Poland where Jewish ghettos were destroyed and the Auschwitz death camp was located.

Dr Kelley commented that Frank developed an almost godlike martyrdom especially when he resigned himself to the fact that he would be found guilty by the court. He told Kelley through Howard: 'Someone must be held responsible. The leaders must pay for the crimes of Hitler and Himmler who escaped.' Frank followed this immediately with a denial of his own personal guilt. Howard knew at this time that Frank had had some hand in his parents' fate because Auschwitz was on his patch. Howard reflects:

'As I sat and chatted with him, this man who had murdered more Jews in Poland than anyone else, seemed anything but a mass murderer. When I studied this calm, sometimes philosophical man it was not possible to tell by looking at him how evil he was. That was true of all the defendants. When these men were taken out of their ordinary surroundings as leaders in Nazi Germany, you could not tell that they were mass murderers.'

During the interviews, Howard had to exercise complete restraint and not display any emotion or desire for revenge. Sometimes it was difficult, but as he rationally and calmly explains: 'there was so much feeling of superiority within me at that time. And gratitude. I was the victor and could give the orders. I couldn't take a knife to Frank, Goering or any of the others and murder them. That would have made me a murderer like them. I had to let justice take its course.'

For Hans Frank, being held in solitary confinement with no one except the occasional remark from a guard, or the visits from Kelley and Howard, or psychologist Dr Gilbert, he had time to reflect philosophically and religiously on life. He was also preoccupied with Hitler's defeat. As Howard translated his remarks and soliloquies, Kelley frantically took notes. Frank declared to them, almost religiously: 'I tell you the scornful laughter of God is more terrible than any vengeful laws of man. Here are the would-be rulers of Germany, each in a cell like this with four walls and a toilet, awaiting trials as ordinary criminals. Is that not a proof of God's amusement at a mass, sacrilegious quest for power?' That was certainly true of Frank himself who said with no shame, 'We must not be squeamish when we hear the figure of 17,000 shot.'

During 1946, Howard and Goldensohn found Frank's moods could swing from great highs one moment to tearful deep depression the next. In his diary, Goldensohn recorded three entries about Frank's pleasure at seeing him and his 'translator'. When they entered his cell at six thirty on the evening of 12 February 1946, Frank had just finished his evening meal after another tedious day in court with the other defendants: 'He was apparently happy to see me and Mr Triest the translator, whom he addressed as "Mr Translator." Frank cleared his cot and chair of clothing, which was strewn about haphazardly, and invited us to be seated. He spoke some English, but I preferred speaking to him in German through the interpreter.'

On 5 March, they visited Frank again and found him engrossed in reading. He looked up as Howard and Goldensohn shuffled into the confines of the cell and sat down. Through Howard, Goldensohn proceeded to ask Frank about his family background and history. It became the subject of several interviews. On this occasion, Frank readily talked about his parents and the past. Goldensohn asked what had motivated him to become an anti-Semite. Frank replied, 'It was because of Germany... I never had a single Jew put in a concentration camp or burned – that I can prove. The extermination of the Jews was a personal idea of Hitler's.' Frank then explained how Nazi Germany had no freedom of press or media and in that sense the only good thing to come out of the trial is that it proved the German people's innocent.

When Howard and Goldensohn visited Frank two weeks later on 16 March, they found him upbeat and pre-occupied with explaining the development of National Socialism. Frank spoke to them about the 'hypnotic personality' of Hitler which drew in everyone around him. Goldensohn wrote of that interview: 'Frank was in one of his cheerful, smiling, effusive moods. He greeted Mr. Triest, the interpreter, and myself warmly and said that he was delighted to have us visit him again.' An entry appeared in the diary for 20 July 1946, in which Goldensohn wrote:

'Frank was in his blue denim coveralls, reading a magazine, when Mr Triest and I entered his cell this morning. It was Saturday and there was no court session. The sun streamed in through the open cell window. Most of the other defendants were exercising in the yard. He was grandiosely courteous and eager for company. As usual he greeted us eloquently, and ceremoniously made place for me on his chair and for Mr Triest on the cot beside him. He filled his pipe with tobacco, an American brand, and praised it highly.'

When Howard and Goldensohn entered Frank's cell on 20 July, Frank was sat on his bed reading a magazine. It was Saturday so the court had recessed for the weekend. Most of the other defendants were out in the exercise yard, taking in some sunshine. Frank expressed his usual pleasure at seeing Howard and Goldensohn, and gestured for Goldensohn to sit at the desk and Howard beside him on the bed. Goldensohn asked Frank what he thought of the judges and the trial, to which Frank replied that they had political motives and were not true lawyers.

That day, Frank was busy preparing his final speech for the court. In a surprising declaration, Frank told Howard and Goldensohn that, even though Hitler was dead, he [Frank] was taking the blame for what had gone wrong. Frank strongly believed that, even in absentia, Hitler should have had a defense lawyer to defend him. He argued with a sense of urgency that the other 21 defendants had lawyers, so why not Hitler too? This, he believed, would prevent the growth of a "Hitler legend".

Hans Frank's ultimate denial of any knowledge of the horrendous crimes under his jurisdiction made Howard feel that Frank was covering his own trail. It seemed nonsensical that Frank could have been completely innocent of the millions of murders on Polish soil. 'Hans Frank was the only one,' says Howard, 'who, while denying some of the crimes- - yes - showed genuine remorse but it could not change his fate.'

RUDOLF HÖSS

As if contact with Hans Frank wasn't challenging enough, the new witness who was brought into the jail in March 1946 was more testing of Howard's personal resolve. Rudolf Höss was not at this point being tried for war crimes, but being held as a key witness at Nuremberg. Justice in respect of his own war crimes would come the following year.

Living in hiding at the end of the war, under the assumed identity of Fritz Lang, he had evaded capture by Allied teams of Nazi-hunters for eleven months. He was finally caught on a farm near Heide in Schleswig-Holstein, northern Germany by a group of German-speaking Jewish refugees serving in the British army. He was eventually brought to Nuremberg Prison and held in isolation in the C wing. Howard's job was to interview him, sometimes on his own, sometimes with Goldensohn. That fateful day in March 1946 when Goldensohn informed Howard that Höss was their new charge, Howard knew the implications. It was known that Höss had committed crimes on a scale which equalled defendants like Hans Frank.

As commandant of Auschwitz, Höss was responsible for the murder of at least three million people, mainly Jews, and had also sanctioned the most horrendous crimes within the camp. Mentally, Howard prepared himself as he approached C wing with Goldensohn, with a slight tremble in his step. The first face-to-face meeting would be the most testing emotionally. How could Howard prepare himself to face the man who had probably sealed the fate of his own parents?

He followed Goldensohn into the cell, sat down and stared at the man who appeared to have no distinctive characteristics. Höss immediately launched into a series of complaints about the chilblains on his feet, stemming from the time he had been in British custody. Howard explains with justifiably no sympathy: 'In the jail, he had no shoes because we had taken away his shoelaces so he couldn't hang himself. Höss demanded his shoes back because his feet were permanently cold. It was all rather pathetic but it was not possible to feel any compassion for him.'

ADMISSION OF GUILT

As Howard interviewed Höss, deep down he knew the bitter truth about his parents' fate and yet clung to the futile hope they somehow they might still be alive. He found Höss to be a man who showed not the slightest remorse for his crimes. In fact, Höss remained boastful of what he had done. On one occasion, Howard entered the cell alone, to obtain information for Colonel Andrus and found Höss in a mood quite ready to talk.

Howard says: 'That day he talked to me quite freely about his crimes. He corrected himself and said to me: "Ah no. I didn't kill two and a half million. I did better than my quota. I killed three million."'

There was nothing Howard could say except sit in silence. Howard believes today, as he did then, that it was best not to give the man the satisfaction of seeing his pain and disgust. Again, Howard says the same of Höss as the other defendants: 'I was surprised by the fact that it was not possible to tell how evil Höss was just by looking at him. It was only by talking to him, and hearing in intricate detail how the extermination program was carried out, that I saw the extent of pure evil.'

Sitting on the bed beside Höss, with Goldensohn scribbling notes at the desk, how did Howard exercise restraint? Where was his anger? His desire to grab Höss and confront him? Over the years, Howard has been asked these questions many times. Today, he is relaxed in his answer:

'I maintained the same self-control towards Höss as I did towards Goering or Hans Frank and the others even though I had an extra reason to hate the man. Sitting so close to him and talking to him was surreal. Maybe that was why I coped with the situation. When I was conversing with him, or any of the other defendants, they seemed like ordinary men but of course they were anything but ordinary.'

Howard harboured an almost numbing disbelief at the scale of the crimes for which Höss was personally responsible. In a moment of silence, while he waited for Höss to answer one of Goldensohn's questions, he tried to come to terms with reality and said to himself, this man killed three million people! It did not quite register: 'Höss looked like any decent human being, much like anyone's kind grandfather. That was the shocking and surprising thing about him.'

With the first painful interview over, Goldensohn indicated to the guard through the tiny open window that they were ready to leave the cell. As the guard unlocked the door, Höss was still complaining about his cold feet. Howard followed Goldensohn out. The guard slammed the door behind them.

Howard turned to Goldensohn and chipped: 'His feet will be a lot colder when they hang him.'

Howard entered Höss's cell on several more occasions with Goldensohn, tasked with translating the most detailed responses about the precise workings of the Nazi death machine. Each time, Howard exercised the same constraint as before, being mature enough to realize that if he made one wrong move his job would be over and face disciplinary charges from Colonel Andrus. That would have meant being sent to the United States. Trying to rationalize may not be the full answer because nothing could change the fact that Howard was coping with multiple trauma at this time: the loss of his home and country of birth, the death of comrades on the battlefields of Europe, and the murder of his parents. In those days, there was no trauma counselling. Howard had to get on with life and hold it all together.

AUSCHWITZ: THE TRUTH

Amongst the most difficult interviews ever carried out with Höss were in April 1946. On 9th April, as the guard unlocked the door, Höss rose to his feet and stood to attention. Goldensohn asked Höss to be seated and he duly obeyed. Höss was still complaining about his cold feet.

Goldensohn steered the conversation to the workings of Auschwitz. It was then that Howard learned the graphic details of what went on in the camp: how Poles were shot if they had been part of the resistance movement, and of hair being removed from the dead bodies of women and sent to factories to be made into fittings for gaskets. With Howard translating, Goldensohn pressed Höss on the question of who had been murdered at Auschwitz.

'Men, women and children, only Jews,' Höss replied. What did Höss think of this? He replied he was only obeying orders from Himmler and it was not possible to question Himmler's orders. Höss tried to rationalize that if the Jews were not exterminated, then Jews would in the end exterminate all Germans. When pushed further by Goldensohn, Höss acknowledged that he had blindly accepted Himmler's orders. He then explained how Auschwitz was almost empty when he arrived there in May 1940. In the summer of 1941, he had been summoned to Berlin to meet with Himmler, where he was given instructions to rebuild Auschwitz to accommodate twenty thousand prisoners and turn it into an extermination camp. Himmler had told Höss: 'The Führer has now ordered the final solution to the Jewish problem. Those of us in the SS must execute these plans.'

Höss had duly returned to Auschwitz to execute Himmler's orders. From his subsequent description to Howard and Goldensohn, it was clear that he carried out orders with alarming efficiency and enthusiasm. Höss organized two derelict farmhouses on the Auschwitz site to be converted into gas chambers for the arrival of the first transports. It was he who took the decision to use Zyklon B gas in the gas chambers.

'How many people at a time were exterminated in each farmhouse?' asked Goldensohn, through Howard interpreting. Höss stared at the floor for several moments in silence. Goldensohn wrote in his diary: 'He then shifted his eyes from me to the floor to Mr Triest, and finally after about half a minute he said, "In each farmhouse eighteen hundred to two thousand persons could be gassed as one time".'

'How often were the gas chambers used?' asked Goldensohn.

Höss replied: 'sometimes two or three times a day, but there could be a gap of three weeks or more between its use. Men were gassed separately from women and children. When transports arrived, SS doctors decided who was suitable for work around the camp and separated them from the rest of the arrivals. The others were marched for nearly a kilometre to the two farmhouses and gassed.'

'Did the prisoners ever panic?' asked Goldensohn.

Höss replied, 'Yes sometimes, but we worked it smoothly, more smoothly as time went on.'

In this lengthy interview, Höss explained how, from 1942, new crematoria with four underground gas chambers were built at the camp and these were used immediately. This now covered the period when Howard's own parents arrived at there from Camp Drancy.

Howard swallowed hard and continued translating as Höss, oblivious to Howard's personal pain and connection, explained the capacity of each chamber. Two gas chambers accommodated two thousand people; the smaller two could take sixteen hundred each. Höss dispassionately described how only those selected for work had their names added to the camp lists of prisoners. All files on those who were gassed were destroyed. This explains the absence of Berthold and Lina Triest's names from the lists which survive in the camp archives. Howard tried to concentrate, his mind all the while piecing together bit by bit his parents' fate.

'Did ordinary Germans know about Auschwitz?' asked Goldensohn. Howard quickly re-focused his attention to translate.

In a monotone voice Höss replied: 'only those who worked there and they had to sign an oath of secrecy. Newspapers were not allowed to print anything about the camps.' Höss then admitted to being present when the gas chambers were used.

'There was no question,' says Howard, 'he knew everything that went on at Auschwitz.'

Goldensohn and Howard visited Höss again two days later. In his diary, Goldensohn records the interview in which he asked Höss what he had been thinking about. Goldensohn wrote: 'He had the usual puzzled, apathetic expression and gazed from me to the wall and back to Mr Triest, the translator, in a doleful manner, and then answered, "I haven't been thinking of anything in particular".'

During that interview, Höss proceeded to speak about his family history, childhood and religion. Goldensohn asked him if he was ever haunted by the memories of the murder of over 2.5 million people. Höss simply replied, 'no'. That figure excluded the other extermination camps of which he was administrator. Höss continued, 'I thought I was doing right, I was obeying orders and now of course

I see that it was unnecessary and wrong. I don't know what you mean by being upset about these things because I didn't personally murder anybody. I was just the director of the extermination program in Auschwitz. It was Hitler who ordered it through Himmler and it was Eichmann who gave me the order regarding transports.'

HÖSS TAKES THE STAND

Howard attended the court proceedings the day Höss took the stand in the courtroom, 'On that occasion Höss was bureaucratic and matter-of-fact,' he says. Howard listened attentively as Höss's affidavit was read to the court. In it, Höss admitted:

'I commanded Auschwitz until December 1, 1943 and estimate that at least 2,500,000 victims were executed and exterminated there by gassing and burning and at least another half million succumbed to starvation and disease. Those who were fit for work were sent into the camp. Others were sent immediately to the extermination plant.'

Of all the Nazi prisoners held at Nuremberg, the astonishing part about Höss's involvement was his sick pride at what he had done. The other defendants might have denied their guilt, remained belligerent or anti-Semitic, but they did not show any sign of pride at their part in the Third Reich.

In his defence, Höss boasted to Howard back in the cell: 'I received the orders. I carried them out. I did them the best I could.'

This same admission came from the other defendants too – Hitler gave the orders. And they obeyed. Howard says, 'It was clear to us then that they blamed Hitler because he was dead and could not deny it.'

How did Howard cope with being in such close proximity to Höss, a man of such evil who had personally decided the fate of his parents? He coped only because he knew that Höss would eventually face the gallows for his crimes. And so he did. After Nuremberg, Höss was handed over to a Polish Military Tribunal for trial. He was found guilty and hanged at Auschwitz on 7 April 1947, on the same gallows used by the Nazis.

Although today Howard claims he felt no bitterness towards the defendants or ordinary Germans at that time, only once has he publicly expressed hatred and that was on a documentary made about his life called *Journey To Justice* (2006). In it, he says: 'When I left Germany in 1939, I hated Germans and everything connected to Germany.'

When pressed further, he slightly modifies what he expressed in his film. The lack of bitterness, Howard argues today, is down to a childhood fantasy when he was thirteen years old. By then he had lived for three years under the Nazi regime. He dreamed of himself returning one day as the victor and driving through the streets of Munich in a white Mercedes. The young Howard also fantasized that he had a huge vacuum cleaner and held it all over Germany and sucked up the bad people. Every bad German, which for him was most Germans, was taken away. All that remained in Germany were empty buildings, the countryside, streets and homes – all the familiar things which made Howard feel secure.

Later on, at the end of the war, these sentiments held true in Nuremberg and his contact with the German population. He wanted Germany rid of its bad Germans. However, he still knew a small number of "good Germans", mainly those who had once worked for his father, but he mistrusted all the others when they told him they had not been Nazis.

Howard says, 'I did feel bitterness towards the Germans and hatred for the defendants at Nuremberg. Not everyone was in the same pot – there were some good Germans. Whether those "good Germans" were truthful to me about their past remained an open question.' When pressed further about the war criminals and exacting revenge, Howard responds with unqualified solemnity and sincerity:

'Emotionally it was difficult at times. You stand in front of the man who murdered your parents. What can you do? I couldn't kill him. That would have made me a murderer too. In most of the cells were men who in some way were responsible for my parents' death. Do I kill them too? Would I go into Hans Frank's cell and kill him too? Frank – the bloody-thirsty governor of Poland? Not only would it make me a killer, but the emotion would ultimately turn in on me and I would end up killing myself. I couldn't kill them *but* I would have liked to have done the same thing to them as they did to millions of innocent people – to see them suffer a long, slow, painful death; to be killed in the same horrific manner that they inflicted on innocent men, women and children, including my own parents. There were those who could not do my job because of their own suffering. On the other hand for me there was so much feeling of superiority, of gratitude that I was now the one who is the victor. I could call the cards and give the orders. They were sitting behind bars. I had my life and freedom. I was 22 years old at that time. We had just won the war. I could ride on a torrent and that enabled me to do my job with the top Nazi defendants. I had to let justice take its course.'

In the end, for Howard, it remained true. For justice was finally done without him having to exact personal revenge. He says levelly: 'Höss was not the only one responsible for my parents' deaths. He was one in a chain of Nazis or Nazi collaborators who carried out mass murder. It was not possible for me to hunt them all down and kill them. The only rational way forward was to allow justice to take its course and trust in that process.' Perhaps the most sobering message from Howard's contact with the two 'beasts of Poland' is his comment, 'any personal revenge could not bring back my parents.'

CHAPTER FOURTEEN

THE MILITARY MEN AND KEY NAZI WITNESSES

ITLER'S FORMER MILITARY men Admiral Doenitz, General Jodl, Admiral Raeder and Field Marshal Keitel were held on the ground floor of the prison. They had a ready answer for the atrocities and the easiest way out by claiming 'we were just obeying orders.' They told Howard: 'We are military men and when Hitler ordered us to do something, we had to do it. We were bound by our military oath.' Or they would say, 'Goebbels told me to do this,' or 'Goering ordered me to do that.' Howard recalls with some cynicism that the higher up the hierarchy the defendant was, it was all Hitler's doing. They usually blamed the leaders who were dead. That effectively meant Hitler and Himmler.

The day the guard unlocked the cell door of 54-year old Doenitz, Howard found Doenitz as proud and aloof as the day he had arrived at the prison. In spite of his formal reserve, Doenitz did not find it beneath himself to sign a book to the prison translator. With dignity, he took the copy of *Die U Bootswaffe* from Howard and wrote: 'In memory Great Admiral Doenitz, Nuremberg January 1946.'

On 3 March, the courtroom showed film reel of Buchenwald concentration camp. Goldensohn was keen to gain some reaction to the atrocities. When the defendants returned to the cells at the end of the day, Howard followed him into the cell of Doenitz. Doenitz was questioned on the evidence which he had seen. 'Of course he couldn't deny what was shown on the film,' says Howard, 'but he saw it as an isolated event rather than part of a wider program of persecution and extermination.' In the coming months, Goldensohn would probe further and ask Doenitz whether he knew about the existence of the concentration camps. 'Yes and no,' Doenitz replied. 'I knew of some from 1933, but I was too busy with naval matters. I knew nothing of the killing of Jews.' What did Doenitz think of the trial? He replied:

'It is a joke. If these trials confined themselves to who ordered killings of the Jews and other killings of human beings, it would be all right. I wouldn't be kept in the dock three hours. But I sit here from November on, and hear the same stuff over and over again. Half the time I no longer listen. I just draw pictures or jot down my musings... The big folly of this trial is that it lacks the two men who are to blame for anything which was criminal, namely Hitler and Himmler.'

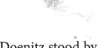

During his questioning and interviews, Doenitz stood by Goering and continued to believe that Goering was not as bad as the prosecution were trying to claim.

Doenitz was a key figure in the Nazi Regime at the end of the war. As Hitler's chosen successor after Hitler's suicide in the Berlin bunker, Admiral Doenitz had immediately retreated to the protected enclave of Flensburg on the German-Danish border. From there, he had arranged Germany's unconditional surrender to the Allies. After his arrest, he always claimed he did not know the other Nazi leaders. He tried to justify and qualify his position by saying that he had barely met them other than on some formal occasions. 'Doenitz was determined to set the record straight regarding his own position,' says Howard, 'and told us he was going to write his own memoirs. He went on about how he took no responsibility for the mass atrocities even though he was Hitler's top naval man. He, Doenitz, knew nothing of the extermination plan for Jews, 30 million Slavs or mass murders in Russia and Poland. Even so, Doenitz was still accused of carrying out unrestricted submarine warfare. Nothing could change his part in that.'

JODL AND KEITEL

At the beginning of the following month, Howard went to see Alfred Jodl, one-time Colonel-General and chief of operations for the German High Command. Jodl's inscription to Howard inside the book *Mit Hitler in Westen* was short. It read: 'A. Jodl, Generaloberst retired 2.2.46.' Leaving Jodl's cell, Howard turned his attention to

Admiral Raeder. He found Raeder cordial in conversation. Raeder wrote inside *Jahrbuch der Deutschen Kriegsmarine*: 'With best wishes E. Raeder, Nuremberg 2.2.46.'

Howard then headed to see Keitel, former Field Marshal who had ordered captured British commandos and SAS men to be shot in cold blood by his Keitel Order. Keitel, not unsurprisingly, justified Hitler's defeat in military terms. He inscribed inside the book, *Jahrbuch der Deutschen*, the words: 'The German army of yesterday has only one purpose – to fight with honour or perish in battle, Keitel, Field Marshal retired.'

The inscription reveals that even in defeat this military leader confidently retained his sense of duty, code of honour and fight to the death, something which was imbued into the German military consciousness. Howard reflects on the military men and says: 'To me, they seemed quite ordinary men sat in their cells. Their kind, gentle faces hid the fact that they were also guilty of crimes on a massive scale because they had sent hundreds of thousands to their deaths by their battle orders and commands.'

THE WITNESSES

While the main defendants spent each weekday in the courtroom, Howard was back in the prison interviewing key witnesses for the trial, some of whom would later themselves stand trial for war crimes. The witnesses were held in a different wing and were called to the trial as witnesses to the atrocities. There were held Margarete Himmler (wife of the deceased Heinrich Himmler) and their daughter Gudrun. Howard and Kelley interviewed them in the cell, during which Himmler's wife was questioned about her late husband's activities. Although the Allied authorities had kept watch on her, she was ultimately not implicated in charges of war crimes.

By February 1946, the following Nazis were being held as witnesses, awaiting interview in the cells by Howard and Goldensohn: Rudolf Höss, Otto Ohlendorf, Oswald Pohl, Sepp Dietrich, Paul Schmidt, Albert Kesselring, Franz Halder, and Ewald von Manstein. Also held were:

> Erhard Milch, Field Marshal and armaments chief of the Luftwaffe, tried at a later court in Nuremberg and given 15 years imprisonment;
> Erich von dem Bach-Zelewski, SS General from 1941, chief of anti-partisan units in Russia from 1943.
> Kurt Daluege, Reichs Protector of Bohemia and Moravia. He was tried in Czechoslovakia and hanged in 1946.
> Rudolf Mildner, Head of Gestapo in Chemnitz and Kuttointz, Poland
> Walter Schellenberg, Chief of Office VI (Secret Intelligence Services) of RSHA from 1942.

Occasionally, Howard accompanied Goldensohn to interview witnesses outside the prison who were not in custody, and that included Goering's wife and daughter, Edda. 'In the case of Mrs Goering,' says Howard, 'we delivered personal items to her from her husband, like a couple photographs and letters.'

THE FIELD MARSHALS

Albert Kesselring, former General Field Marshal and Supreme Commander of the German armed forces in Italy, was an important witness at Nuremberg. His was a rank below Reich Marshal which was held by Hermann Goering. The sixty-year old Kesselring was interviewed by Howard and Goldensohn in early February 1946, having first spent time under interrogation at the London Cage in Kensington Palace Gardens, London which had become the War Crimes Interrogation Unit (WCIU). Kesselring told Howard and Goldensohn that no soldier under his command committed any crimes or atrocities. He claimed to suffer from amnesia and dizziness due to a past fractured skull.

When interviewed by Howard and Goldensohn on 12 March, he was asked about art treasures looted from the Abbey of Monte Cassino in Italy and delivered to Goering. Kesselring replied that he thought the treasures were in the Vatican. Goldensohn went on to ask about the bombing of Rotterdam. Kesselring maintained that throughout the war he only ordered the bombing of military targets, not civilian places or cultural and historic sites. He was reminded by Goldensohn of the Keitel Order of 16 December 1942 about dealing with partisans in Italy; how partisans which included women and children, should be shot if captured. Later, Keitel issued an order to arrest a significant number of the male population amongst the partisans "… and in the event of an act of violence being committed these men will be shot."

Kesselring was held culpable for his role in the army. He was tried by a British military court later in 1947, was given the death sentence, but this was reduced to life imprisonment.

In C wing, Colonel Andrus was also holding eight Field Marshals and Generals who were initially brought to Nuremberg as witnesses. Howard and Goldensohn were engaged in interviewing them while the main defendants were otherwise occupied in the courtroom. While at Erlangen, Howard had acquired a copy of the book *Soldaten*. Inside the front cover, each of the eight military witnesses penned their signature and rank:

> Gerd von Rundstedt, Field Marshal, 28.5.46
> Guenter Blumentritt, General of the Infantry, 28.5.46
> von Brauchitsch, Field Marshal (no date)
> von Kleist, Field Marshal (no date)
> von Manstein, Field Marshal (no date)
> von Leeb, Field Marshal, 20.6.46
> Halder, Generaloberst, 21.6.46
> List, Generalfeldmarschall, 24.6.46

Back in the cells in C wing were various other Field Marshals and Generals, including Sepp Dietrich, 54-year old head of the Hitler Bodyguard regiment, SS General and commander of the Sixth Panzer Army from 1944 until 1945. He was originally captured by American forces and brought to Nuremberg prison. He protested that he was not a member of Hitler's inner circle but was only involved with him on official business. Howard and Goldensohn entered his cell to question him about his relationship to the Führer. Dietrich told them he last saw the leader on 25 February 1945.

'How did he look?' asked Goldensohn. 'Sick. Almost completely finished,' replied Dietrich. When questioned about atrocities, Dietrich argued that the mass execution of Russians was purely propaganda on the part of the Allies to discredit Germany. He claimed that as a Catholic, he himself was not anti-Semitic as borne out by his belief that the solution to the Jewish problem should have been to allow Jews to leave en masse, aided as much as possible by the Third Reich.

Other witnesses interviewed by Howard and Goldensohn included former Field Marshal Erich von Manstein, later sentenced by a British Military Court and imprisoned. Albert Kesselring, Field Marshal of the Luftwaffe and Supreme Commander of German forces in Italy, was tried in Venice by a British Military Court; and Franz Halder whom Hitler had dismissed in September 1942 for opposing the German offensive on Stalingrad. Halder made an attempt on Hitler's life in 1944 and spent the rest of the war in Ravensbrück concentration camp.

SS AND DEATH SQUADS

Another witness at the original trial was Walter Schellenberg who had been in Counter-Espionage, the Chief of Secret Intelligence Services of the RSHA, then head of the SS. He would later receive a prison sentence for his crimes. The witnesses were visited less often than the main defendants and, as such, kept their distance from Howard and Goldensohn. In their responses about war crimes and their own part in them, witnesses like Ohlendorf and later Rudolf Höss often appeared more ruthless than the main defendants.

Otto Ohlendorf, head of security services of the Reich Security Main Officer and Commander of the death Squads (*Einsatzgruppe*) on the Eastern Front, was questioned by Goldensohn about his role in the orders to liquidate Soviet Jews. Ohlendorf proceeded to describe in detail the rounding up and shooting of Jews. In a matter-of-fact way with no sign of remorse he told Howard and Goldensohn that he had been informed that 90,000 Jews were shot, including children but he reckoned the figure was nearer 70,000.

'He confidently analyzed his figures,' says Howard, 'and told us it was about 5,000 a day for a year. Ohlendorf explained his position by telling us he did not personally carry out the shootings but gave the orders to the death squads.' So Ohlendorf justified his actions by claiming he could not disobey orders from above. He went on to explain that if he had not carried out the killings, someone else would have done it for the regime. He maintained that lives would not have been saved by his refusal to carry out orders. This marked a totally new line of argumentation. Rather than disobey his leaders, Ohlendorf understood his role to ensure the killings were carried out in a *humane way*. Howard could not believe the coldness and audacity of the man. He recalls:

'As I translated his responses, a chill ran through me. By now, I should have been used to anything, having already heard so much in the cells. But still there were shocks for us. Did he expect us to feel that his approach towards humane killings exonerated him?'

Otto Ohlendorf was sentenced to death at a later Nuremberg hearing in April 1948 and hanged on 8 June 1951.

Another witness brought into the prison was former *SS Obergruppenführer* Oswald Pohl who arrested by British forces on 27 May 1946. Pohl had built up the Nazi administration in the 1930s as chief in the SS and towards the end of the war was responsible for the administration of the concentration camps and SS industrial enterprises. Goldensohn questioned him about his background and family. Pohl explained how he had been sought out by Himmler as early as 1933. He gave assurances to Howard and Goldensohn that he would tell them everything and hold nothing back.

In an interview in June 1946, they learned how gold teeth from victims of the concentration camp were sent to Pohl's office on Himmler's direct orders. Pohl said he never handled the goods himself because his task was the administration of the camps, which he carried out efficiently according to Himmler's orders. Pohl was therefore adamant that he had no part in the killing of Jews. Taking charge of the administration of eleven concentration camps did not in his eyes make him guilty. For him, administration had nothing to do with Hitler's extermination program. Pohl believed that the Jewish problem should have been solved for Hitler and Germany without extermination. He told Goldensohn through Howard:

'If I were really an anti-Semite, I would have hated
Jews – but I never hated them. All I did was follow
orders. My conscience is clear. I never ordered the
death of a Jew or personally killed one.'

Pohl's solution to the Jewish problem was to deny the Jews
their jobs and homes, and thus drive them out of Germany,
without a need to kill them. In this way, Pohl denied any
responsibility for the acts of the other Nazi leaders.

The questioning of Pohl then turned to his views on
the forced labour of Russians in the camps, especially
in Landsberg which Goldensohn had visited just before
the end of the war. Pohl responded that he himself had
nothing to do with the Landsberg camp. He told Howard
and Goldensohn that there were several hundred labour
camps all over Germany and he could not visit all of them
to regulate conditions. In this way, too, he could argue that
he was not responsible for conditions in the camps. The
Allies had too much incriminating evidence on Pohl to
free him. Pohl found himself in the dock at a subsequent
Nuremberg trial and was sentenced to death. On 8 June
1951, he was hanged at Landsberg prison.

FACING THE PAST

Occasionally, figures from Howard's past came to
Nuremberg and sought him out, maybe with a guilty conscience to put their minds at rest about the past. During
1946, visitors included Mr Povel who had purchased
Berthold's factory in the summer of 1938, and his man-
ager Mr Dittmann who had survived the war in spite of

being half-Jewish and married to a Gentile. From their visit, Howard learnt that his father's old factory at 2-4 Mueller Strasse had been subjected to Allied bombing and could no longer be used. Povel was running the business from different premises. Povel tried to convince Howard that he had paid an honest price for the factory and that Berthold Triest had got what he wanted for it.

Povel and Dittmann asked Howard if he harboured any resentment or bad feeling towards them. Howard assured them that he did not. This was in part due to the fact that, as he admits, he was 'riding on top of the world as part of the occupying American forces.' What did he want with a few rooms in a factory? Howard was now an American soldier and American citizen. Munich held nothing for him materialistically that he wanted to save from his past.

Before he said goodbye to Howard, Povel asked if he could have a can of gas because their vehicle had run out. One thing Povel knew was that the Americans were not short of certain supplies. Six decades later, Howard can look back on the irony of that moment and say, 'the young Jewish lad whose father had been forced to sell out to the big German industrialists, gladly gave them a can of gas.'

It is clear that part of Howard's ability to deal so well with the pain of the past comes from his year spent at Nuremberg. In the cells, he faced the past head on. That has to have made the difference to his psychological healing. On a daily basis, he came personally close to those who had destroyed his life in Germany and murdered his parents. It provided an immediate and personal form of closure which other victims of the Holocaust did not experience, including those who served in different units of the American forces.

Of the two psychiatrists, Howard became closer to Goldensohn, partly because they worked together for much longer than with Kelley. But also Goldensohn took a genuine interest in Howard's past. The two men become friends over the seven months that they worked together. Goldensohn expressed a desire to see Munich and the places of Howard's childhood. One weekend, Howard and Goldensohn drove to Munich together. They walked the sites of Howard's childhood and saw for themselves the textile factory which had once belonged to Berthold Triest and was now bomb damaged. The devastation from Allied bombing was as bad there as other major German cities.

As they explored old haunts, Howard was able to explain how his father Berthold was a proud German veteran of the Great War who had served from August 1914 to February 1919 as a Field Hospital inspector and been awarded the Iron Cross. Howard stood with Goldensohn outside the former artist's apartment at 2-4 Manhardt Strasse where he was born twenty-three years earlier. So much had happened in the intervening years. Re-living the memories and the past with Goldensohn, a psychiatrist, must have contributed to the emotional journey and healing process for Howard.

Chapter Fifteen

NUREMBERG: THE VERDICT

THE ARCHITECTS OF the war were dead: Hitler, Goebbels and Himmler, but the Nuremberg Court would ensure the other defendants paid for their part in the crimes. Now July 1946, after nine long months, the trial proceedings were over. The world had been presented with evidence for the worst atrocities in human history. Now it awaited the verdict on the twenty-one defendants who were deemed responsible for heinous war crimes. The psychiatrists had done their job and ensured the men had been fit to stand trial.

Dr Leon Goldensohn left Nuremberg on 26 July 1946, the day the final speeches were given to the courtroom by US Chief Justice Jackson and British Prosecutor, Sir Hartley Shawcross. In his speech that day, Chief Justice Jackson told the court: 'If you were to say of these men that they are not guilty, it would be as true to say that there had been no war, there were no slain, there has been no crime.'

Howard remained at the prison on various duties for Colonel Andrus until October. The defendants faced just over two months of isolation in their cells before the verdicts would be decided.

On 1 October 1946, the courtroom convened for a final time to read out the verdicts. The Court was told by Sir Hartley Shawcross that all were guilty of 'common murder in its most ruthless form', but the sentences would vary for some of them:

- Hermann Goering: guilty on all 4 counts. Death by hanging
- Julius Streicher: guilty on all 4 counts. Death by hanging
- Rudolf Hess: guilty on counts 1 and 2. Life imprisonment
- Joachim von Ribbentrop: guilty on all 4 counts. Death by hanging
- Ernst Kaltenbrunner: guilty on counts 3 and 4. Death by hanging
- Alfred Rosenberg: guilty on all 4 counts. Death by hanging
- Hans Frank: guilty on counts 3 and 4. Death by hanging
- Wilhelm Frick: guilty on counts 2, 3 and 4. Death by hanging
- Walther Funk: guilty on counts 2, 3 and 4. Life imprisonment
- Karl Doenitz: guilty on counts 2 and 3. Ten years imprisonment Erich Raeder: guilty on counts, 1, 2 and 3. Life imprisonment
- Keitel: guilty on all 4 counts. Death by hanging
- Baldur von Schirach: guilty on count 4. Twenty years imprisonment
- Fritz Sauchel: guilty on count 3 and 4. Death

by hangingAlfred Jodl: guilty on all 4 counts. Death by hanging
- Artur Seyss-Inquart: guilty on counts 2, 3 and 4. Death by hanging
- Albert Speer: guilty on Counts 3 and 4. Twenty years imprisonment
- Baron von Neurath: guilty on all 4 counts. Fifteen years imprisonment
- Hans Fritzsche: not guilty
- Hjalmar Schacht: not guilty
- Franz von Papen: Not guilty.

Martin Bormann, Hitler's secretary and successor to Rudolf Hess, was sentenced to death *in absentia*. The Allies did not know then that he had already committed suicide and that his body lay under the ruins of Berlin. It was not until 1972 that the remains of his body were discovered in the city.

Three defendants, Hjalmar von Schacht, Franz von Papen and Hans Fritzsche were found not guilty and freed by the court. It was to be a bitter sweet freedom. In spite of the verdict, they walked out of the prison complex to a hostile reception by the German people and feared for their lives. They found a world deeply embittered by thirteen years of a brutal Nazi regime. The world was not ready to receive them as free men.

Albert Speer, Erich Raeder, Karl Doenitz, Walther Funk, Baron von Neurath, Baldur von Schirach and Rudolf Hess received prison sentences. Hess served his sentence of life-imprisonment in Berlin's Spandau prison and died there in 1987 in his nineties. Ironically

Hess's paranoia was proved wrong because he lived the longest and no one poisoned him, although conspiracy theories have since suggested that he was assassinated at that time by the British or American Secret Service. The other eleven defendants were sentenced to death by hanging.

GOERING'S LAST ACT

On 16 October 1946, the hangmen prepared the gallows at Nuremberg for the eleven men. None of the defendants were informed when the executions were to be carried out. For sixteen days they waited. They were finally told the exact time of their fate just hours before the scheduled hangings. The executions were to take place during the night, on gallows specially constructed in the prison gymnasium. In an unexpected last minute move, one man evaded justice. Goering had one final surprise in store for Colonel Andrus. After the verdicts were delivered by the court and the sentences read on 30 September 1946, Goering had made a request to be shot according to military code. His plea was denied. He returned to his cell where psychologist Dr Gilbert awaited him. Gilbert asked him about the verdict.

Goering looked pale, his eyes popping. 'Death!' he replied.

Dr Gilbert records: 'he dropped on the cot [bed] and reached for a book. His hands were trembling in spite of his attempt to be nonchalant. His eyes were moist and he was panting.' Gilbert was then asked to leave the cell.

All the best efforts to keep a constant watch on the defendants could not prevent a determined Goering from committing suicide just hours before his hanging. Prison staff rushed into his cell but it was too late to prevent fatal effects of the cyanide pill. While Howard was not present for the hangings, because he had just been transferred to Military Government in Munich, he kept up with the final days of the accused at Nuremberg.

Rumours circulated at that time that the cyanide pill was given to Goering by an American prison guard who had befriended him over the course of his time in the jail. A Texan and former hunter, the guard came to admire Goering the hunter. Since he and Goering shared a passion for the sport, it gave them common ground during the extraordinary period in the prison. If true, this growing friendship had possible consequences in the final days of the trial. It was believed that Goering gave the guard his expensive gold watch in exchange for a cyanide pill. What use was the watch to a condemned man? A cyanide pill was far more valuable. Ultimately, no one really knew for certain how Goering obtained that fatal pill.

Howard comments: 'Goering's suicide broke Colonel Andrus who felt personally responsible. There was a feeling that like Hitler, Himmler and Goebbels, Goering had escaped any form of justice by taking his own life.'

The other ten men faced their fate and were hanged by executioner John C. Woods. Julius Streicher remained anti-Semitic to the end. His last thoughts and fanatical words were ironically for the Jews. From the gallows, he shouted the words 'Purim Fest 1946', a mirror reference to the biblical event of the suffering of the Jews in the time of Esther and Purim over two and a half thousand years earlier. Streicher knew the Bible well.

After the hangings, to prevent conspiracy theories, each defendant's body was photographed as evidence to the world that they were dead. The bodies were taken under armed guard to Dachau concentration camp where they were cremated in the same ovens that had killed thousands of Jews. It is believed that the ashes of the condemned men were, ironically, taken to Munich's Isar River and scattered there – the same river that Howard and his father had walk along during the pogrom against Jews on 9/10 November 1938, and the same river in which Berthold's WW1 dagger and helmet had been cast.

Although Howard had left Nuremberg before the hangings, he comments: 'I did not personally see the men hang, but I saw pictures afterwards. I was glad that at least we had eliminated some of the evil from the world but, in my estimation, not enough of them.'

In summing up his experience of Nuremberg, Howard says: 'None of them, however relaxed and open they were with us, confessed to being guilty. They could not see the wrong they had done. Whatever they said in the prison cell, we listened. Some of their stories made very little difference to their situation – certainly it did not change their fate. And I never once felt sorry for them.'

THE LASTING IMPRESSION OF NUREMBERG

It was to be the figures of Hermann Goering and Julius Streicher who made a lasting impression on Howard.

Howard would live forever in the shadow and pain of the Holocaust and the shadow of the figures responsible for it. They left an indelible, if uncomfortable and painful, mark on Howard's psyche. But of all the defendants, it is the memory of Julius Streicher which continues to haunt him over six decades later:

> 'Although I became closely connected to all the defendants and came to know them well, I did not warm to any one of them. The defendants stood united in disowning the killing machine and saying they were following orders. They felt that the only reason they were on trial was because they had lost the war, not because they had committed terrible things. They may appear larger than life as far as history is concerned but they certainly did not offer a picture of superiority. They were ordinary men and some looked very pitiful. When I think back to the one who was the nicest to me and who treated me the best, it was Streicher – the biggest Jew-baiter of all time. That does not mean that I ever grew to like him, but Streicher seemed to like me and trusted me. They all did, but him most of all.'

Howard had been in Nuremberg prison for the whole duration of the trial as a witness to the process of justice. He poignantly concludes about that chapter of his life:

> 'There is little doubt that Nuremberg was the most extraordinary period of my life. I finally came face-

to-face with the men who sent six million Jews, including children, to their deaths, along with five million others. To have the perpetrators in their prison cells at last and see justice done was terribly important to me. I had had the experience of being there at the end of the war when Munich was taken by our American forces, then sitting with the heads of the former Nazi government in Nuremberg prison itself and finally with Military government for another year in the city of Munich where I was born, and where I was assigned to denazification work. It was a complete turn-around. The persecuted young man returned to the city of his birth. He who had lost most of his family in the Holocaust, who probably would not have wanted to go back to Germany, was now suddenly the conqueror, the hero, the liberator.'

Perhaps the biggest irony of Howard's experience was that Julius Streicher went to the gallows unrepentant, never knowing that his 'Aryan friend' at Nuremberg was Jewish. And in another twist of irony, twelve years later in 1958, psychiatrist Dr Douglas Kelley committed suicide by biting a cyanide pill – just as Hermann Goering had done. When Howard learnt the news about Kelley, he felt complete shock: 'The exact reason for Kelley's suicide was always unknown. It was thought to have been severe depression after family difficulties. In subsequent years I often wondered whether Kelley acquired the cyanide pill during his time in Nuremberg. Who knows? He was a doctor and could have had access to it.'

CHAPTER SIXTEEN

POST-WAR MUNICH

HAVING WITNESSED JUSTICE and spent a year working in the prison in extraordinary circumstances, Howard left the city of Nuremberg in the autumn of 1946. He was transferred to Munich for duties with Military Government. In a twist of fate he returned to the city of his birth as a member of the occupying Allied forces to play his part in the process of restoring democracy to Germany. His life had come full circle.

Germany lay in ruins from Allied bombing. Berlin was almost totally devastated, as was Munich. A whole nation had been brainwashed for thirteen years by a dictator whose racial policies led ultimately to the death of six million Jews and eleven million others in concentration camps and death camps. Adolf Hitler had turned upside down a civilized nation and destroyed the fabric of its intellectual and cultural life, committing genocide on an unparalleled scale. Nazism had been crushed; its surviving leaders brought to justice.

What remained was the difficult and delicate task of removing all traces of Nazi ideology from German society and administration and the restoration of democracy. It was a huge undertaking and one the Allies could ill afford to get wrong if they were to avoid the mistakes made at the end of the First World War. Rebuilding the infrastructure and social and civic fabric alongside the implementation of democratic fell to them. Howard was to be part of that denazification process.

Having lived through the Nazi regime for six years and been part of its crushing defeat, Howard returned to live for a year in the city he once called home. Munich was now a very different place. It had lost his family, its Jewish population and its soul. Desolate barren wilderness of rubble and ruins from Allied bombing mirrored the desolation and despair in Howard's heart. It was obvious that his parents had not survived. They were no longer part of the once-familiar Munich life of his childhood. Life could never be the same again. Howard also learnt from his maternal grandmother Rosa that his paternal grandfather Moritz Triest had died in Theresienstadt in 1942 at the age of 92. Munich's once vibrant Jewish community of 9,000 to 10,000 members when the Nazis came to power in 1933 had disappeared. During 1938 around 3,500 emigrated.

On 21 November 1941, the first deportation of a thousand Munich Jews had taken place. They were sent to Lithuania and all shot five days later. There were 43 further deportations from Munich before May 1945, with as many as 3,000 being murdered by the Nazis. These figures do not account for families like the Triests who left Munich and were deported to the death camps from other countries. Of the Munich Jewish community, only 300 survived the camps to return after the war.

MILITARY GOVERNMENT

Howard was assigned to G2 Unit of the Intelligence Section of Military Government Bavaria. The office was located on Munich's Tegernseer Landstrasse in a large complex of buildings occupied by the Headquarters of the Office of Military Government Bavaria. Some of the immediate staff with whom Howard worked included his friend Britt Bailey from Nuremberg, also Peter Beer, Narvid, Steingut, Burkardt and Wohlbier. It was a long time ago and Howard today does not remember their full names. Howard's work involved various aspects of denazification duties, including organizing the trials of former Nazis in the villages, small towns of Bavaria and Munich itself. His office compiled weekly intelligence reports which came in from various places. The reports were analysed by Howard and colleague Peter Beer, a former Austrian refugee in the US army. Key information of importance was extracted from the reports and sent on to the higher army authority.

In Munich, as elsewhere in post-war Germany, the Nazi past was quickly buried in the rubble that was being cleared from the city. A whole nation had blanked thirteen years of Nazi ideology and brain washing. During Howard's work in denazification, the civilian population was quick to reassure him that they had never been Nazis and had taken no part in Hitler's persecution of the Jews. They took him to one side to influence his view of their past. He was shown photos of old Jewish friends and told stories of how they themselves had not been anti-Jewish towards Germany's Jews. Those who knew Howard's family sent their condolences.

'Again, as in my previous visits to the city, it was very difficult to find anyone that had ever been a Nazi. They all denied it. Who had run the country?' Howard says with some sarcasm. 'The collective disavowal of the crimes committed seemed to characterize a whole nation.'

It left Howard numb and in disbelief. Germany would have to recognize its part in the crimes if any reconciliation were to be possible.

During this phase of his post-war work, Howard took the initiative to record conditions in the city. He used a 16mm camera to shoot a silent black and white film of Munich. The movie camera had originally come from a German observation place and been exchanged for two packets of cigarettes. Cigarettes were "the currency" in Allied occupied Germany, in contrast to the devalued German Mark. Howard took the film to be processed by Agfa Company about a quarter of a mile away from the headquarters of Military Government. One other film of Munich exists for this period, taken in 1945 by another American soldier. Apart from Howard's movie, there is nothing for 1946 or 1947 during the American occupation of Munich. His film is significant because it shows the progress made since 1945 in the reconstruction and clearing up the city after its complete destruction in the war. Being young, he did not think about the film's importance for history's sake but as evidence to show the state of Munich to his uncle and other relatives back in the United States. A copy now exists in the Munich city archives. Howard had always been interested in film and photography, something which he took up as a career later in civilian life.

Living for a year in Munich meant that childhood memories were an ever present reality for Howard. He could little escape the past all around him, whether the atrocities for which the defendants had been tried at Nuremberg or meeting again people from his early life. Walking down once familiar streets now in a state of some disrepair, he felt the loneliness of a life without his parents, his extended family and friends. His grandmother Rosa was the only member of the family now living in the city. Recalling this period for the biography, Howard reveals himself to be a person who has never been afraid to confront the past, however painful that might be. In Munich, as in Nuremberg, he confronted the past head on.

CHAPTER SEVENTEEN

A LIFE IN THE SHADOW OF NUREMBERG

I N OCTOBER 1947, with his duties with Military Government complete, Howard left Munich to return to America to take up civilian life again. By now, he had gained full American citizenship. He boarded a train to Bremerhaven on the morning of 1 October 1947. After a few days in an army camp, he took a ship bound for New York. As the ship carrying Howard and 800 other passengers neared the coast of America, his sister Margot had already boarded a flight from Detroit bound for New York to greet him at the port on his arrival. She had left Switzerland to take up a new life in the United States and was lodging with their uncle Kurt, as was their grandmother Rosa, the survivor of Theresienstadt. America had welcomed, and given shelter to, the only surviving members of the Triest family.

Howard arrived in the port of New York on 15 October. It felt reassuring to be back on American soil. After two days together in New York, Howard and Margot flew back to Detroit. Howard felt he could settle down and start living a normal life. 'It was like coming to America for the first time and starting all over again,' he comments.

In December 1949, he received a letter from the Department of the Army in Washington with a letter attached from the White House and signed by President Harry Truman. In it, the President thanked the personnel who had been involved in post-war duties in Germany from 1945. Truman expressed his personal thanks and 'of the nation, for the achievements of Military Government in restoring and preserving the peace in Germany and in resisting fearlessly and successfully the blockade of Berlin.' Truman went on to say, 'I wish to have all those who assisted in this great effort receive recognition by their country for the contribution which they have made to the peace of the world… I am sure history will find that the unprecedented relationship established between victors and vanquished has indeed strengthened the peace of the world.' Howard feels justifiably proud to have played his part in that process.

The employment before Howard had enlisted in the army had been a temporary one. He now had to consider whether to study to train full-time for a profession or find employment. In the end, he took up a main job and studied part-time, using a small sum of $300 received on discharge from American forces. For about a year, he took whatever work he could, mostly odd jobs in Detroit and a short time in Chicago as a travelling salesman selling sports clothing and ski wear. At the end of 1948, he left Chicago to return to Detroit to join his uncle's large children's wear store.

Howard managed the store for a number of years, but deep down his love of movie-making persisted. He decided to start a business in filming weddings, special events and parties at weekends. Then he changed to branch into commercial and travel movie-making; something which he found creatively rewarding. He then joined Guardian Photo Division, a division of Guardian Industries, one of the world's giant glass makers. Howard became their training director of Guardian Photo and Guardian Industry until his retirement in 1985.

FAMILY LIFE

At the end of 1949, a few days before New Years Eve, Howard went out on a blind date in Detroit to meet a woman who would become his wife. She was Anita Hammerstein from a Detroit Jewish family and seven years younger than Howard. After the success of the blind date, Howard invited her out again for New Year's Eve but she was otherwise engaged. They met on New Years Day instead. Three months later, in March 1950, they became engaged. On 30 July 1950, they were married in a synagogue according to the rites of the Jewish tradition. Their first son, Brent, was born on 23 June 1952 and second son, Glenn, on 29 March 1960. Howard and Anita have four grandchildren and one great-grandchild.

In 1958, Howard and Anita went on their first joint visit to Europe which included the city of Munich. Howard came unexpectedly face-to-face with the past again when he walked into the bank to change money: 'I saw a man who was familiar. We looked at each other. Then I realized that he was my headmaster at the Handelsshule back in 1937. He remembered me well and my mother. He told me about my teachers, most of who had died in the war. He was retired by then. I could not help but wonder: had he been a Nazi? Would he have told me if I had asked?'

JOURNEY TO JUSTICE

In 2003, Howard took a journey with his son Brent to the significant places from his childhood and the Nazi period for a documentary film to be called *Journey to Justice*, which came out in 2006. During their visit to Munich Howard arranged to meet with an old school-friend Hans Fischach from the Gebeleschule. He hadn't seen Fischach for seventy years.

Howard knew Fischach had a Nazi past. Fischach had broken off their friendship when he enrolled in the Hitler Youth in the 1930s. Fischach and Howard's lives went their separate ways. Fischach was protected; Howard had to flee for his life. Both had once lived on Munich's Reitmorstrasse. For the filming in 2003, they met in the apartment where the Triests had once lived. How would Hans Fischach explain the past? As is shown in the documentary Howard graciously greeted Fischach but Fischach was quick to quote to him words from Goethe's Faust: "Politics is an ugly song and that is how it is."

In a further attempt to deal with his Nazi past, Fischach showed Howard a book which he had written about his youth. The book makes virtually no reference to Nazism. Fischach then passed Howard a letter from a former Jewish acquaintance who apparently liked the book, as if that made everything fine. Howard comments, 'It was clear that Fischach had buried the full truth about his past.'

Fischach had attended an elite Führer school and proudly showed Howard a photograph of himself in uniform. He had joined the German army's SS Panzer Division, was wounded in action three times in Normandy and lost the sight of one eye. Many Jewish families living in apartment block at 53 Reitmorstrasse where Howard and Fischach grew up, had perished in the Holocaust. That included Howard's own grandfather and parents, and the Kaplan family. These were families who had been German for generations. Howard is quite blunt when he says:

> 'Fischach expected and would have been happy for Germany to win the war. He disassociated himself from the Jewish families and neighbourhood where he grew up and denies ever being a Nazi or anti-Semitic, even though he became a Nazi Officer in the German forces.'

Howard knows exactly how he feels about meeting Hans Fischach after seventy years. He is under no illusion that: 'Fischach would be a National Socialist if Germany had won the war, as would 80-90% of Germans. We spoke as friends, as we did before the Nazi regime took over the course of our lives, but somehow we had completely blacked-out the bad times.' Fischach handed Howard a copy of his book and inscribed inside:

> In memory of our grand meeting
> (After 75 years!) with my old friend Heinzi
> With best wishes, from the heart.
> Yours, Hans Fischach

Does Howard feel on a personal level that he and Fischach were reconciled? Howard says: 'I am realistic enough to realize that Fischach knew exactly the path he was taking during the Nazi regime.'

However, when pressed about Germany as a nation today, Howard says that he is reconciled with Germany and the past. Maybe it is that sense of reconciliation which enabled Howard to meet with another visitor during his time in Munich in 2008 – Nicolas Frank, the son of defendant Hans Frank. When Nicolas learned that Howard was in the city, he asked to meet him. Howard agreed. They met in a hotel room.

Nicolas Frank was only six years old when his father was hanged in Nuremberg. He is one of the few children of Nazi war criminals who have grown up hating his father for what he did. Howard and Nicolas had a good heart-to-heart during their meeting and are in touch from time to time. Nicolas Frank's father's words at Nuremberg are still hauntingly prophetic today:

> 'We fought against the Jewish people for years and we indulged in the most horrible utterances as my own diary bears witness against me. A thousand years will pass and still this guilt of Germany will not have been erased.'

True as this might be, in terms of justice, the last word cannot go to Hans Frank, the beast of Poland who was responsible for millions of deaths. The prerogative of having the final word must go to Howard himself…

When Howard was reunited with his sister, Margot, at the end of the war, together they vowed to honour their parents' memory by celebrating life. Today, on the site of Camp Drancy outside Paris, a memorial marks the spot where the entrance to the camp once was. It is a physical reminder that from here over 70,000 Jews were deported to the gas chambers of Auschwitz. Drancy was the last location where Lina and Berthold Triest were known to be alive. In synagogues or specially designated places in America, France and Germany, memorials have been erected to the Jews of Munich, and in some cases Lina and Berthold Triest are mentioned by name. What of commemorating them? Howard replies: 'the biggest memorial is in my heart.'

THE LEGACY OF NUREMBERG

Nuremberg has become a blue-print for the future and its legacy far-reaching for international justice. The trial influenced the development of international criminal law, with trials still being held in The Hague for war criminals of other conflicts today. Importantly too, Nuremberg became a model for The Universal Declaration of Human Rights (1948); The Genocide Convention (1948); and the Geneva Convention (1949).

Like much about the Second World War, Nuremberg has passed into almost mythological status in history. There is a continued fascination with the rise and fall of Hitler and Nazi Germany that does not appear to abate with time. However for Howard, it is the memories of the liberation of Buchenwald that continue to haunt him in a way that his experiences of Nuremberg do not. Every time he looks at photographs of the death camps he searches the faces of the survivors for his parents. Even though he knows they died in Auschwitz, still he instinctively looks for them amongst the haunting eyes staring back. He says he will search until the day he dies.

For Howard Triest, living in retirement in Florida in the United States, Nuremberg is ever present in his memory on a daily basis. Time does nothing to erase his extraordinary experience. Through a twist of fate, he survived Nazi Germany to become a witness to justice and part of history in the making.

SELECTED BIBLIOGRAPHY

The vast majority of the material for *Inside Nuremberg Prison* is based on interviews with Howard Triest.

Andrus, Burton. *I Was The Nuernberg Jailer*, Tower, 1969

El-Hai, Jack. *The Nazi and the Psychiatrist: Hermann Goering, Dr Douglas M. Kelley and a Fatal Meeting of Minds at the end of WWII*, Public Affairs: 2013 Fry, Helen. *The M Room: Secret Listeners who Bugged the Nazis*, Thistle, 2015

Fry, Helen. *Churchill's Secret Soldiers*, Thistle Publishing, 2015

Fry, Helen. *Denazification*, The History Press, 2010

Fry, Helen. *Churchill's German Army*, The History Press, 2009

Gilbert, Gustav. *Nuremberg Diary*, Da Capo Press, 1947, reprinted 1995

Goldensohn, Leon. *The Nuremberg Interviews*. Pimlico, 2007

Hansen, Horace R. *Witness to Barbarism*, Thousand Pinetree Press, 2002

Kelley, Douglas. *22 Cells in Nuremberg*. Greenberg Publisher, New York, 1947

Neave, Airey. *Nuremberg*, Coronet Books, 1982
Owen, James. *Nuremberg: Evil on Trial.* Headline Review: 2006

Documentary: "Journey to Justice" by Steve Palackdharry (2006), narrated by Brent Triest, and still photography by Glenn Triest.

ACKNOWLEDGEMENTS

This book would not have been possible without the dedicated support and patience of veteran Howard Triest. Howard is a remarkable man, humble yet proud to have played his part in some of the defining moments of history. He has been available for countless hours of interviews over an eighteen month period. I feel extraordinarily privileged to be entrusted to tell his story and love his sense of humour. Huge special thanks to Howard's wife Anita for her belief in this book, her patience and support during the whole process. Also huge thanks to their sons, Brent Triest and Glenn Triest, for their practical help and encouragement. Glenn very kindly designed the jacket cover for the book.

Howard's sister Margot has been a vital part of the process of writing this book. She has helped with providing crucial information and eye-witness accounts. A debt of thanks goes to her for enabling me to include parts of her story in the book. I could not write any of my books without the constant support, practical help and encouragement of my family and friends. Huge thanks go to them: my husband Martin, our three sons Jonathan, David and Edward, and my mother Sandra.

To my closest network of friends, which include my dynamic writing partner in historical fiction James Hamilton who is always there for me as a creative and for sharing in the process. Also to my dear friends Jane McAdam Freud, whose art and sculptures are an inspiration and her husband, Pete Hansen. Also to Brana Thorn & Frank Gent, Daphne & Paul Ruhleman, and Louisa Albani. My thanks too my hardworking agent, Andrew Lownie for all his support of my work.

ABOUT THE AUTHOR

Historian and biographer Helen Fry has written over 20 books on the Second World War, as well as aspects of Anglo-Jewish history. Her books include: *The M Room: Secret Listeners who Bugged the Nazis in WW2*; *Spymaster: The Secret Life of Kendrick*, *Churchill's Secret Soldiers, From Dachau to D-Day, Freuds' War, Denazification,* and *German Schoolboy, British Commando*. She is an Honorary Research Fellow at the Dept of Hebrew & Jewish Studies at UCL. In fiction, under the pseudonym JH Schryer she has co-written novels with James Hamilton: *Goodnight Vienna* and its sequel *Moonlight over Denmark,* and *Erin Manor*. Helen has appeared on the Channel 4 documentary *Spying on Hitler's Army* (2013), ITV's *Britain's Secret Homes* (2013); Channel 5 for *The Hunt for Hitler's Missing Millions* (2014); and interviewed live in the BBC studio with Huw Edwards in Normandy for the 70th anniversary of D-Day, 6 June 2014. She is frequently interviewed on radio, both national and regional. A member of the prestigious Biographers' Club, she can be found on Facebook and Twitter. Her official website: www.helen-fry.com